KOREA TRIANGLES 1945-2020

TREADING A TIGHTROPE

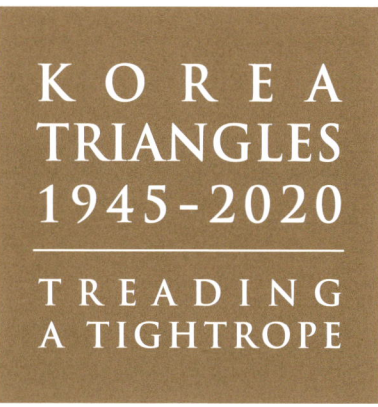

KOREA TRIANGLES 1945-2020

TREADING A TIGHTROPE

Essays by HAN SUNGJOO

THE ASAN INSTITUTE for POLICY STUDIES

KOREA TRIANGLES, 1945-2020
TREADING A TIGHTROPE

Essays by **Han SungJoo**

First edition June 2020

Published by The Asan Institute for Policy Studies
Registration number 2010-000122
Registration date September 27, 2010
Address 11, Gyeonghuigung 1ga-gil, Jongno-gu, Seoul 03176, Korea
Telephone +82-2-730-5842
Fax +82-2-730-5849
E-mail info@asaninst.org
Design by EGISHOLDINGS

ISBN 979-11-5570-212-3 93340

Copyright © 2020 by The Asan Institute for Policy Studies.

All Rights reserved, including the rights of reproduction in whole or in part in any form.

Printed in the Republic of Korea

Han Sung Joo

Han Sung Joo is a professor emeritus at Korea University. He previously served as the minister of foreign affairs and ambassador of the Republic of Korea to the United States. He was also UN Secretary-General's special representative for Cyprus, a member of the UN Inquiry Commission on the 1994 Rwanda Genocide, and chairman of the East Asia Vision Group. He is currently chairman of the Asan Institute for Policy Studies.

He is a graduate of Seoul National University and received a Ph.D. in political science from the University of California, Berkeley. Previously, he taught at City University of New York and was a visiting professor at Columbia University and Stanford University. He was also a distinguished fellow at the Rockefeller Brothers Fund and acting president of Korea University.

Table of Contents

Acknowledgements — 08

Preface — 09

Chapter 1 — **The Emerging Triangle I: Korea and China in Historical Perspective** — 16

- Early China-Korea Relations — 16
- Consequences of the Korean War (1950–53) — 19
- The Road to Normalization — 22
- China and South Korea: Approaching a New Century — 23
- China-Korea Relations and the Other Major Powers — 26
- Some Concluding Observations — 27

Chapter 2 — **The Emerging Triangle II: The U.S.-Korea Relations** — 30

- The Early Decades: A Slow Start — 31
- Post-Independence Relationship — 32
- South Korean Relationship with the United States in the Post-Korean War Period — 37
- South Korea-United States Relations in the 1960s — 42
- Bilateral Relations in the 1960s — 43
- Korean Reaction to Carter Troop Withdrawal Plan — 50
- Korea-U.S. Relations in the Post-Park Period — 59
- Korea and the Carter Administration — 60
- The Reagan Administration's Korea Policy — 65
- The North Korea Question — 71
- Future Perspective — 74
- Conclusion — 76

Chapter 3 — The Emerging Triangle III: The North Korean Nuclear Issue — 80

North Korean Policy Toward the United States and Nuclear Weapons — 80
Nineteen Months: The North Korean Nuclear Crisis of 1993–94 — 82
Fast Forward, 2020 — 88
North Korea, Today — 92
The Korea Focus: The Influence of the Major Powers — 93
A New Triangle Takes Shape: Korean Attitudes Toward the U.S. and the PRC — 97
The Unification Question — 99
Conclusion — 101

Chapter 4 — An Uneasy Triangle: Korea Between China and Japan — 104

The Geopolitical Situation in Northeast Asia — 105
Korea's Role in China-Japan-Korea Triangle — 106
The Northeast Asia Triangle and North Korean Nuclear Issue — 108
Rise of China and Resurgent Nationalism in Northeast Asia — 110

Chapter 5 — Division Management and Unification: Korea vs. Germany — 120

Status of Inter-Korea Relations — 122
Possibility for Duplication? — 123
Persuading Major Powers — 124
China's Interests and Reasons for Its Stance — 126
Conclusion — 134

Chapter 6 — A Grand Strategy for South Korea? — 136

The Regional Landscape: South Korea and the Major Powers — 138
Strategic Choices — 145
Conclusion — 147

Afterword — 148

Index — 152

Acknowledgements

I would like to respectfully dedicate this book to two of my erstwhile teachers when I was doing my graduate work in the United States. They are: Professor John T. Holden of the University of New Hampshire who supervised my M.A. thesis; and Professor Robert A. Scalapino of the University of California, Berkeley, who was the chief advisor for my Ph.D. dissertation.

For the publication of this book, I am indebted to three other persons in particular. They are Dr. J. James Kim, senior fellow at Asan Institute for Policy Studies; Mr. Jang Jae Jin, president of Egisholdings, a design company in Seoul, which specializes in book design; and Ms. Song Ji Eun, program officer of the publication department at the Asan Institute. Dr. Kim gave an excellent editorial help which has made the book more coherent and readable. Mr. Jang is responsible for making the book more handsome and giving it a book-like appearance. Ms. Song set right any possible inconsistencies in the book that might have been left unsorted out and capably dealt with the odds and ends but critical elements of a difficult and complicated publication job.

Preface

This book is a review of the changing relations among Korea (North or South Korea after division of the country in 1945), China, Russia/USSR, the United States, and Japan. These dynamic and evolving relationships can often be seen as triangular patterns of varying dimensions. The first section will focus on China-Korea relations, the ties that date back the farthest. In fact, China maintained a dominant relationship with Korea for nearly two millennia right up until the end of the 19th century. Then, after a half-century of hiatus, China re-emerged on the scene during the Korean War to become a staunch supporter of the northern half, a relationship that would last through the 1980s. Since the early 1990s, however, China opted to pursue a "two-Koreas" policy rather than continue an exclusive relationship with Pyongyang. Twenty years later, China went back to tilting toward North Korea. Thus, since 1992, when China established normal diplomatic relations with South Korea, it has come to have a presence on the peninsula that is as strong as any other country including the United States.

The United States, for its part, became involved in Korean affairs almost by chance in the late 19th century. But the U.S.-South Korean alliance that developed after the Korean War of 1950–53 has proven to be a lasting and effective one. Together, the trans-Pacific allies have competed quite successfully with the Sino-North Korean alliance for nearly half a century. Now the United States is making an effort to catch up with China in establishing ties with both Koreas. The one obstacle to achieving this objective is North Korea's continued refusal to give up its nuclear weapons and long-range missiles. Once this problem is resolved, the result could be the United States competing with China for a large presence on the Korean peninsula. This subject, the United States-Korea relations, will be the focus of the second section.

The North Korean nuclear issue is one that involves all the powers of the region and their policies and politics as well. It also informs how the dynamics of the triangular relations among China, the United States, and the two Koreas impact on relations between the two Koreas. This will be the launching point for the third section of this book which focuses on South Korea's position between China and Japan.

The final essay deals with issues related to the Korean unification question. It discusses the history of the division and prospects for reunification. The essay on unification discusses why each of the stakeholders of the Korean question will either support or oppose Korea being reunified and, if it accepts such an eventuality, under what conditions.

The conclusion that will be drawn in this book is that this is all, in essence, a process by which several triangles merge into one multi-angular relation, so that each of the major powers involved in Korean affairs formulates its policies in the context of several triangular relations involving the other powers as well as Korea itself. As a result, they are coming to perceive Korea as one point of the diplomatic triangle. The three major powers—the U.S., China and Japan—also find that each is involved in another triangle together with each of the two Koreas of the divided Korea. Will this bring some of them, the United States and China, for example, head to head with each other over the Korean Peninsula? Or will there be a new kind of relationship in which the three actors maintain a healthy distance from one another and manage a peaceful and cooperative existence? The jury is still out on this question. But we could start by understanding how these triangular relationships have evolved to date.

In his book on post-Cold War geopolitics, *The Grand Chessboard*, the late Zbigniew Brzezinski underscores the existing and potential rivalry in Asia between China and the United States.[1] According to Dr. Brzezinski, China regards America as the perpetrator of this rivalry. "Through its Asian presence and support of Japan," he explains, the United States "stands in the way of China's external aspirations."[2] He goes on to make the interesting assertion that the focal point of this Sino-American rivalry will be Korea. Although this assertion may be going too far, there is much truth in the

---

1. Zbigniew Brzezinski, *The Grand Chessboard: American Primacy and Its Geostrategic Imperatives* (New York: Basic Books, 1998).
2. *Ibid.*, p. 159.

notion that the two powers are intensifying their competition. Where will this competition lead?

In human relationships a triangle often means two persons in love with a third one at the same time, creating tension, jealousy, and often trauma. In diplomacy, though, the term triangle is used to describe a special dynamic among three nations such that considering only bilateral relations among them is inadequate to understand the dynamics between and among them. In recent history, three types of triangular relations stand out. The first is one that seemed to characterize the relationship among the United States, the Soviet Union and China in the 1960s and 1970s. During that period, the three powers alternately competed and cooperated with one another, all the while maintaining a certain distance from each of the others. One might picture a sort of equilateral triangle in this case.

A second type of triangle can be found today among the United States, China and Japan. In this instance, the triangle is an uneven one in that the United States and Japan are much closer to each other—militarily, economically, and diplomatically—than either is to China. Yet, certain elements that link the three powers stop this situation short of being a relationship in which the United States and Japan find themselves together pitted against China. A third triangular-type relationship could be found during the 1960s and 1970s when Vietnam as a small country was caught between two giants—the Soviet Union and China. In fact, this situation was described by Donald Zagoria as "the Vietnam triangle."[3] In an analogous way, North Korea tried to take advantage of the Sino-Soviet rivalry of the 1960s by playing one off against the other. In both cases, a small state got squeezed or tried to maneuver, as the case may be, between two much larger powers.

The relationship among China, the United States and the two Koreas—North and South—presents yet another, still evolving triangular pattern, one which has seen significant changes particularly in the past one decade since 2010. Until the end of the 1980s, China and the United States each had close and exclusive relationships with the separate halves of Korea.

---

3. Donald S. Zagoria, *Vietnam Triangle: Moscow, Peking, Hanoi* (Cambridge: Pegasus, 1967).

Since around 1990, however, an overlapping pair of triangles has emerged—one between China, North Korea and South Korea on the one hand, and the other between the United States and the two Koreas. However, a closer look at the situation suggests a still newer phenomenon—the emergence of a single, more powerful triangular relationship that encompasses China, the United States and all of the Korean Peninsula. This new pattern is developing as both China and the United States are beginning to see the Korean Peninsula not only as a geographical area which houses two Koreas, but also as a place where a reunified Korea may be located sometime in the future although the possibility seems to be remote for now.

Another possible analogy to the Korean situation, although strictly speaking not a triangle, would be the case of Northern Ireland. There, conflicting parties, at least in the past, had their respective supporters—Britain for the Protestants and Ireland for the Catholics. And still another conflict situation of a similar nature is Cyprus. There, the Greek Cypriots are supported by Greece and the Turkish Cypriots by Turkey. There is a key difference between these two cases and the Korean situation: With both Northern Ireland and Cyprus, the patrons and clients are of the same community—whether it is ethnic, religious or cultural. With North and South Korea, however, their respective supporters are there primarily for strategic reasons, and secondarily for ideological reasons. What this means is that the patron-client relationship affecting the Korean Peninsula is not as strong or durable as that in Northern Ireland or Cyprus. Thus, Korea is witnessing what used to be a two-sided conflict between two sets of allies evolving into a multi-sided conflict and cooperation.

However, one advantage that both Northern Ireland and Cyprus have over the divided Korea in alleviating the feud between the two sides is the existence of a larger integrated political entity called the European Union. Despite its limitations, the EU can ultimately serve as a mechanism to amalgamate them into a much larger political community diluting the sense that one side is taking over the other.[4]

---

4. For Northern Ireland, however, the on-going process of "Brexit" complicates the already confusing patron-client relationships even further.

Preface

Korea, because of its geopolitical condition as a country surrounded by powerful and ambitious neighboring powers, has experienced triangular relationships for many centuries, particularly between China and Japan. Through that kind of history, Koreans have acquired both the mentality and know-how regarding how to deal with the geopolitical triangles. Sometimes they came out more intact than other times. Until 1900, Korea had had to recognize Chinese suzerainty through centuries. In the first half of the 20th century, Korea was colonized and ruled by Japan for 35 years. Afterwards, it became a divided country. The division has lasted for 75 years (until 2020) without the Koreans knowing when and whether they would be reunited. Throughout its centuries-long history, triangles of powers related to Korea have kept emerging and evolving. Essays in this book describe the politics of Korea triangles and how Koreans have handled them, particularly during the post-World War II period of 1945–2020.

These "essays" are a collection of slightly edited versions of texts I prepared over several decades—my commemorative lectures, book chapter contribution, conference keynote speeches, and a concluding chapter written specifically for this volume. As such, they were written at different times and on situations of different periods in history. Therefore, the realities and circumstances of each "triangle" may be different and specific depending upon when the essay was written and what period it is dealing with. All of the essays were written during the 40-year period of 1980 to 2020.

However, there is one thread that goes through the whole volume. It is the theme that Korea as a nation and Koreans as a people have had to go through and meet the challenge of walking and treading a tightrope of the triangular relationships they were engaged in among the surrounding powers and have had to find a way to survive and thrive. The essays will hopefully tell how well they have done, are doing, and will do.

Han SungJoo, Seoul, Korea
March, 2020

Chapter 1

The Emerging Triangle I: Korea and China in Historical Perspective

Early China-Korea Relations

Consequences of the Korean War (1950–53)

The Road to Normalization

China and South Korea: Approaching a New Century

China-Korea Relations and the Other Major Powers

Some Concluding Observations

Chapter 1

The Emerging Triangle I: Korea and China in Historical Perspective[5]

Early China-Korea Relations

Throughout history, China has always had close ties with Korea—all or at least a significant part of it. As early as the 2nd century BC, the former Han Dynasty of China established four colonies (known as Hansagun) in the northern part of the Korean Peninsula. In the 7th century, AD, with the help of the Tang troops, Shilla defeated the other two of the existing three kingdoms, Baekje and Goguryeo, thereby establishing for the first time a unified state in the Korean Peninsula. In the 10th century a tributary relationship was established between the Liao Dynasty of the Jurchens and the Goryeo Dynasty in Korea—a relationship that would last in its basic form through successive Chinese dynasties—Sung, Yuan, Ming, and Qing—and their respective Korean counterparts, the Goryeo (918–1392) and Joseon (1392–1910), until 1895.

The historical Sino-Korean tributary relationship was severed after the end of the Sino-Japanese War of 1894–95. At this point, under the Treaty of Shimonoseki, China renounced its suzerainty over Korea and recognized

---

5. Edwin O. Reischauer Memorial Lectures, Harvard University, April 1, 1998.

her "full independence." For the next half a century, Chinese influence in Korea all but disappeared as a result of Korea's domination by Japan. The only exception was Chinese support of the Korean independence movement in China. The KMT (Kuomintang) and CCP (Chinese Communist Party) helped their respective client groups, the Korean Restoration Army on the one hand, and the communist-oriented North China Korean Volunteer Army and the Northeast Anti-Japanese United Army (in which Kim Il Sung served as a division commander) on the other.

Between 1945 when Korea was liberated from Japan and 1950 when the Korean War broke out, China played only a minimal role on the divided peninsula. For one thing, China itself was engulfed in a civil war between the KMT and CCP. Korean returnees from China reflected their former associations, as many in the southern part were supported by the KMT while their northern counterparts were supported by the CCP. Nonetheless, it was the United States and the Soviet Union that exercised overwhelming influence on the peninsula, allowing China's two contending forces only negligible roles there.

The start of the Korean War in 1950 brought China back as a major player, primarily in North Korea, until the late 1980s. China's role in the start of the Korean War remains controversial. Some say that China was an active participant in the planning. Others maintain that Beijing was pretty much left out of the process while the invasion was plotted between Kim Il Sung and Stalin. Documents recently made available suggest that, at a minimum, Mao Zedong was aware of the invasion plan and might have given a tacit approval. It is clear, however, that Beijing's priority at that time was to complete its own civil war against Chiang Kai-shek by taking over Taiwan.

Once the Korean War was underway, though, there is no question about China's central and critical role in the conflict's outcome. Without Chinese intervention, Kim Il Sung would have been driven completely off the Korean Peninsula while Korea was unified under the government led by Syngman Rhee. And after the war, but for China's continued involvement in Korean affairs, North Korea would have become a semi-protectorate of the Soviet Union, somewhat analogous to the Soviet-East German relationship.

Why did China decide to send in her troops during the Korean War? Foremost in Chinese thinking must have been strategic concerns. At the outbreak of the war, Beijing was angered by U.S. President Truman's decision to send the Seventh Fleet to the Taiwan Straits. Truman also decided to send air and naval support for South Korea even before the U.S. ground troops were committed as a part of the UN effort. Then, on October 7, 1950, U.S. forces under UN banners crossed the 38th parallel despite a concentrated diplomatic effort on the part of China to prevent such an outcome. The North Korean forces, already weakened and in disarray, crumbled and retreated quickly, and the UN troops advanced toward the Yalu and Tumen River borders. Just as Truman was motivated to enter the Korean War in large part by the concern that the communists would expand beyond Korea, so was China's decision motivated by fear that the United States would not stop at the Korean border but would threaten China itself. Mao felt the need not only to maintain a buffer between China and the United States but also to deliver a decisive blow to U.S. advances in Asia. Mao must have judged that this was necessary for an eventual takeover of Taiwan.

Beyond these strategic concerns, a second factor in China's involvement stemmed from Beijing's need to maintain ideological and revolutionary solidarity with Moscow, particularly in relation to North Korea. Although there were elements of mistrust and misgivings between Beijing and Moscow, Mao still looked upon Stalin as the senior partner in their common ideological struggle. In this context, North Korea represented both a junior partner and an important experiment. In a recent book on China-Korea relations, Chae-Jin Lee speculated that: "Had China not intervened, China would have lost an opportunity to assume a leadership role in Asian revolutionary movements as well as damaged China's international status and encouraged counterrevolutionary elements in China."[6]

A third and related factor in Chinese participation could have been the traditional and cultural elements in their attitude toward neighboring

---

6. Chae-Jin Lee and Doo-Bok Park, *China and Korea: Dynamic Relations* (Stanford: Hoover Institution Press, 1996), p. 151.

countries. For centuries, China had played a "protective" role toward its weaker neighbors including Korea, preventing them from being dominated by other powers. Mao and his colleagues must have felt China had an obligation to assist North Korea in its struggle for survival.

There were at least two additional factors that allowed, if not encouraged, China to intervene in the Korean War. One was the promise that Stalin gave Mao—a promise later reneged—that the Soviet Union would provide an air umbrella to the Chinese territory, military supplies, and fighter planes. The other was the ambivalent and somewhat complacent attitude of the United States toward the possibility of China's entry into the Korean War-theater. The seeming lack of resolve to stop Chinese military involvement gave the Chinese leadership a tacit assurance that the United States would not react by (nuclear) bombing of China even if the Chinese forces crossed over the Yalu. China eventually succeeded in pushing the advancing UN troops back to what is now the DMZ (demilitarized zone), 12 albeit at great human cost. As a result, China not only became one of the signatories of the Korean Armistice in 1953, but also established itself as the major influence in North Korean politics and foreign relations in the years to come.

Consequences of the Korean War (1950–53)

The Korean War had several significant consequences for the China-Korea and China-U.S. relationships. The first was an enmity between China and the United States which would last almost 20 years until 1972. Together with the Soviet Union, China became an object of America's containment policy and endured nearly a 20-year embargo.

A second consequence is that the United States became a clear and determined obstacle to China's desire to "liberate" Taiwan. The United States signed a security treaty with Taiwan in 1954, and the U.S. Seventh Fleet was routinely deployed in the area. Even after the Sino-American rapprochement of 1972, the United States continued to sell arms to Taiwan and to provide a protective umbrella as demonstrated during the Taiwan Straits crisis in the fall of 1995. At that time China launched missiles to international waters off Taiwan, and the United States responded by sending an aircraft carrier and other naval vessels as a warning to China of the U.S. resolve to protect Taiwan.

Another direct consequence was the postponement of the PRC's admission to the United Nations. During the Korean War, the UN declared China an aggressor. Thus, until 1972, the PRC was locked out of that forum, making it impossible to gain Taiwan's seat, much less become a permanent member of the Security Council.

For the Korean Peninsula, the most important consequence of Chinese participation in the War was that China's influence over North Korea was firmly established. The Soviet Union, which initially approved the North Korean invasion of the South, was hesitant to be involved for fear of confrontation with the United States. By contrast, the PRC not only contributed troops and suffered heavy casualties during the conflict, but also continued to provide support and security by stationing its troops there at least until 1958. These actions inevitably gave China considerable influence in North Korea.

The relationship between China and North Korea was a checkered one, however, as Pyongyang tried to play a balancing act between China and the Soviet Union. Kim Il Sung, who feared the increase in power of the pro-Chinese elements in North Korea, purged them shortly after the Korean War. North Korea was irritated by both the Soviet Union and China during the 1956–58 period, the Soviet Union because of its de-Stalinization campaign and China because of the excesses of the Great Leap Forward movement. Following the withdrawal of the Chinese troops in 1958, Pyongyang moved closer toward the Soviet Union until 1961. During the second half of the 1960s, Pyongyang was particularly upset with China when, in the heat of the Great Cultural Revolution, Kim Il Sung and his government were pictured and denunciated as Stalinist revisionists.

Pyongyang became uneasy in the early 1970s when both the Soviet Union and China sought detente and rapprochement respectively with the United States. It was the "betrayal" of the allies, in response to which Pyongyang decided to seek accommodation with Seoul in 1973. Despite all these periods of coolness, however, China remained a staunch supporter of North Korea. Under the treaty of friendship, cooperation and mutual assistance it signed with the North in 1961, China went on to provide support whenever it was called for.

The reasons for this "special relationship" were clear. For China, North Korea served several purposes. First it was seen as a buffer between the U.S.-dominated South Korea and China itself. Understandably, China considered that with North Korea it had a "lips and teeth" relationship. Second, North Korea was an important prize in its rivalry with the Soviet Union. Thus, Pyongyang was able to take full advantage of the Sino-Soviet conflict in this particular game of triangular politics. Third, in a political sense, North Korea was like a younger brother to China and represented a showcase that would enable China to demonstrate its leadership in the socialist world, particularly in Asia.

For North Korea, its relationship with China was special because China represented one of its two major allies in its struggle against the United States. After the end of the Cold War, and when Pyongyang could no longer take advantage of the Sino-Soviet conflict, China was proven to be the only backstop in its slide toward economic and political bankruptcy and the last supplier of essential commodities such as food and energy. For this reason, Pyongyang hoped and expected that, even in the post-Cold War age of big power reconciliation and accommodation, China would stand firmly behind the DPRK by not recognizing the government of South Korea.

Indeed, despite the changes in big-power relationships, there was not much movement for several years in the two triangular relationships of Beijing-Pyongyang-Seoul and Washington-Seoul-Pyongyang. In fact, there was a 20-year lag between the thaw among the big powers and realignment in the relationship between the major powers on the one hand and the two Koreas on the other. The effects were not felt in Korea until 1991 and 1992 when the Soviet Union eventually "switched sides," and China "shifted its ground," as the eminent journalist Don Oberdorfer described in his 1997 book, *The Two Koreas: A Contemporary History*.[7]

---

7. Don Oberdorfer, *The Two Koreas: A Contemporary History* (London: Little, Brown, 1997), p. 145.

The Road to Normalization

Normalization of relations between China and the Republic of Korea did not happen overnight, however. Starting from the early 1980s, there was a series of events which gave China both the diplomatic opportunity as well as need to deal with South Korea. The first was what might be called "hijack diplomacy." In 1983, six armed Chinese civilians hijacked to South Korea a Chinese airliner containing 105 crew members and passengers. A negotiation between the Chinese and South Korean authorities ensued and the passengers and crew together with the aircraft were returned to China. A memorandum signed by both sides contained Chinese acknowledgment of the "Ministry of Foreign Affairs." For the first time, China acknowledged de facto South Korea's governmental authority.

The second episode might be described as "torpedo boat diplomacy." In 1985, a mutiny on a Chinese navy torpedo boat drifting toward South Korea, gave the two countries another opportunity for inter-governmental negotiations. As a result of negotiations between Xinhua News Agency and the South Korean consulate general in Hong Kong, and to the satisfaction of the Chinese government, South Korea turned over the torpedo boat with its crew members (including the mutineers). In return, the Chinese Ministry of Foreign Affairs delivered a memorandum of apology to the South Korean government.

Then, there was "conference diplomacy" by which South Korean officials attended UN sponsored conferences in China, first on aquaculture, in 1983, and later on Palestine issues in 1985. The Asian Games of 1986 and the Olympic Games of 1988, both of which were hosted by South Korea and to which China sent large contingents of athletes, gave the two countries further opportunities for contacts and exchanges.

In 1991, so-called "APEC diplomacy" provided South Korea and China the chance to deal with each other directly. In the 1991 APEC annual meeting held in Seoul, a formula was devised by which both the PRC and Taiwan (as well as Hong Kong) became members of the regional organization. Finally, in August 1992, China and South Korea officially normalized diplomatic relations.

What prompted China to "abandon" North Korea and recognize the

South? In the larger scheme of things, the end of the Cold War and Sino-American accommodation made it unnecessary for China to view South Korea as a member of the enemy camp. Furthermore, a change of priorities within China made economic considerations more important than either political or military interests. Thus, it appears that the foremost reason for Beijing to seek normalization with Seoul was economic. China had to recognize that South Korea was emerging as an economic powerhouse with which it could expect rapid growth in trade and investment.

But China's economic interest in South Korea went beyond trade and investment. Beijing was particularly interested in the "South Korean model," whose success it attributed to the "developmental authoritarian" government maintained by Seoul during the earlier stages of its economic takeoff. China obviously found South Korea a far more attractive partner in economic development than North Korea.

Still another reason for Beijing's decision to establish full diplomatic ties with Seoul—a decision that apparently received approval from Deng Xiaoping—was the fact that the Soviet Union had already normalized relations with South Korea. This move both opened the way for and compelled China to act in order not to be left off the South Korea bandwagon.

However, before China could take the big step of formal recognition, there were two hurdles to overcome. One of course was strong objections from North Korea, and the other was the fear that, by adopting a "two-Koreas" policy, China might be compromising its own "one-China" policy. Beijing succeeded in overcoming both obstacles. To coax Pyongyang to accept the inevitable, China sent a high-level delegation that included Foreign Minister Qian Qichen. He argued that China's diplomatic normalization with South Korea would help the North in establishing diplomatic relations with both the United States and Japan. At the same time, Beijing was able to side-step the inherent discrepancy between a two-Koreas policy and a one-China policy by exacting a pledge from the South Korean government that it would accept and abide by the one-China principle.

China and South Korea: Approaching a New Century

Since diplomatic normalization in 1992, relations between China and

South Korea, especially in the economic arena, have expanded rapidly. Trade volume, which was barely over $8 billion in 1992, reached a high of $20 billion (one-third of trade volume with the United States) by 1996–97. South Korea became the 4th largest exporter to China and 5th largest importer of Chinese goods. In turn, China became the 3rd largest market as well as exporter to Korea. By 1997, South Korea became the 4th largest investor in China with a total commitment of $4.5 billion. Thus, from China's point of view, South Korea became a major trading partner as well as an important source of investment and technology. Furthermore, for South Korea, China was a country with whom it had a substantial trade surplus (about $4 billion in 1997).

How are China-Korea relations affected by the "IMF situation" [Korea's foreign currency crisis of 1988–89] in South Korea? Obviously, the Chinese leadership must be attentive to what these latest events mean to the "Korean model" of development, which they have been emulating either consciously or unconsciously. Second, Beijing might be concerned about implications for future investment between the two countries, at least in the short term. Finally, China must be wondering about the impact of the foreign currency crisis in several Asian countries, including South Korea, on the regional economy and in particular on the economy of China itself.

In any case, beyond the economic statistics, there have been various other indicators of improving relations between the two countries. South Korea and China have exchanged military attaches and delegations. An aviation agreement was signed. Beijing managed to look the other way when Seoul reestablished relations with Taipei. There were high-level visits, most notably of Presidents Kim Young-sam to China and Jiang Zemin to Korea. And the number of Korean visitors to China increased rapidly—nearly doubling every year since 1992—to a high of about 600,000 in 1996, making the two-way number of visitors some 700,000. Another factor that contributed to the expansion of relations—economic as well as social—is the presence of a large number (about 2 million) of ethnic Koreans in China.

For China, South Korea's main importance has been economic. But for South Korea, China is important country for both economic and political reasons. As the only country with any real influence over North Korea,

China has played a crucial and constructive role in times of crisis. Even before diplomatic normalization, China routinely served as the messenger between Pyongyang on the one hand and Washington and Seoul on the other. And the positive role that China played in connection with the North Korean nuclear issue will be discussed later.

China is also important as a signatory of the Armistice Agreement that ended the Korean War. At present, China finds itself caught between Pyongyang which insists on terminating the Armistice in favor of a peace treaty with the United States on the one side, and Washington and Seoul which argue that the Korean Armistice should be abided by until it is replaced by an alternative peace structure. China, for its part, has tried to take a balanced position on this issue. At the request of Pyongyang, China withdrew from the Armistice Commission to the disappointment of both South Korea and the United States. On the other hand, China has been a rather enthusiastic participant of the four-party talks jointly proposed by Seoul and Washington to come up with a satisfactory alternative.

Another, graphic, example of China's political role in inter-Korea relations concerns the defection in 1997 of Hwang Jang-yop, secretary for international affairs of the North Korean Workers' Party. Despite North Korean protests and entreaties to hand him over, Beijing ultimately allowed Hwang to go to South Korea, albeit by way of the Philippines. Many other North Koreans, although less prominent, also use China as their escape route. How China treats North Korean defectors will have very significant implications, not only for China-South Korean relations, but also for the future fate of the North Korean regime.

In some ways, the very survival of the North Korean government depends upon Beijing's generosity and indulgence. Already China has been providing large amounts of food and energy to North Korea, and Beijing is likely to pick up the slack if the assistance of the international community falls short of the necessary minimum to keep the North Korean regime alive. China accounts for some 70 percent of DPRK's meager oil imports. Thus China is in a position literally to make or break the North Korean regime, a matter of great consequence for South Korea as well.

China-Korea Relations and the Other Major Powers

While China's role regarding the Korean peninsula seems fairly comprehensible, Beijing's policies toward other major powers as they pertain to the two Koreas are less transparent. On this issue, opinions tend to fall into three categories. The suspicious view regards China as a potential threat to the rest of Asia. Those who hold this view argue that with growing economic power, China will strengthen its military capabilities so as to be able to throw its weight around. They emphasize the need for the rest of Asia, together with the United States, to counter-balance Chinese ambitions.

The second view is more benign, and regards China as basically a peaceful nation minding its own business and concentrating on its internal development. Furthermore, according to this view, those who emphasize the Chinese "threat" do so because they need an object of containment to replace the Soviet Union of the previous years.

A third view, eclectic and more realistic, is that it is premature to assume that the future role and policies of China have already been determined. Those holding this view believe China's future attitude and actions will depend very much upon the evolution of China's domestic situation—political and economic—as well as on the response and policies of the outside world toward China. In this sense, the outside world may be in danger of bringing about a self-fulfilling prophecy by stressing the future dangers and threats posed by China.

One issue on which China has shown a high degree of sensitivity is the U.S.-Japan Joint Security Declaration of 1996 and the 1997 guidelines for defense cooperation. Although China recognizes that the continuing U.S. security commitment to Japan has a restraining effect on Japan's rearmament, it nevertheless expresses concern that the United States might be condoning a possible regional military role for Japan. China might be genuinely concerned that the U.S.-Japan security arrangement may actually be part of the presumed "containment" of China. It could also be worried about the remilitarization of Japan. The sensitivity shown by the Chinese leadership on this issue might also be related to domestic politics.

But whatever China's concerns, they have not prevented Beijing from seeking better relations with both the United States and Japan. Such a policy of good neighborliness is also reflected in China's rapid improvement of relations with Russia. This trend should be approved and encouraged. Engaging China with the rest of the world, particularly with the other major powers, is an effective way of encouraging China to play a constructive role in regional peace and security.

This is especially true when it comes to Korea. China's outlook, including its relationships with the United States and Japan, as well as Korea, will have a crucial impact on the evolution of events on the peninsula. In fact, as a signatory of the 1953 Korean Armistice and participant in the four-party talks, China's role is critical in Korea's pre-unification, unification, and post-unification stages. The position that China takes on the issue of a continued U.S. troop presence in Korea, for example, will certainly be a factor in determining U.S. policy on that vital issue.

Some Concluding Observations

In sum, in the 21st century, China will strive to secure the international status and position it thinks it deserves. Whether China will want to go well beyond that is an open question. The answer perhaps depends upon how it is treated by other powers and whether it is welcome in the mainstream of global relations. For its part, China should recognize and adapt to the changing nature of international relations. This means shifting from an approach that emphasizes domination and hicrarchy of power to one that thrives on interdependence and international pluralism. With the help of enlightened policies on the part of both China and its neighbors, China can establish the kind of trusting and cooperative relationship with the outside world that will enable it to play a constructive role in the Asian hemisphere in the century to come.

Chapter 2

The Emerging Triangle II: The U.S.-Korea Relations

The Early Decades: A Slow Start

Post-Independence Relationship

South Korean Relationship with the United States in the Post-Korean War Period

South Korea-United States Relations in the 1960s

Bilateral Relations in the 1960s

Korean Reaction to Carter Troop Withdrawal Plan

Korea-U.S. Relations in the Post-Park Period

Korea and the Carter Administration

The Reagan Administration's Korea Policy

The North Korea Question

Future Perspective

Conclusion

Chapter 2

The Emerging Triangle II:
The U.S.-Korea Relations [8]

After yesterday's survey of Korea-China relations, my story today is a fairly modern one. But it's every bit as important. It begins in 1855, when four American sailors jump a shipwrecked whaling vessel and wash up on Korea's shore. The ship was called "Two Brothers," and although it was not then apparent, the name must have been fortuitous, as this represented the earliest encounter between Koreans and Americans. A less innocent and better-known engagement took place a decade later when another American vessel, the USS *General Sherman*, wound its way deep up the Taedong River near Pyongyang. The Americans proceeded to kidnap a local official, and the Koreans retaliated by burning the ship and massacring its officers and crew.

Now, leap across a century and more. It's July of 1995. "We are truly blood allies," Korean President Kim Young-sam observes on the eve of an official visit to Washington, D.C. "Ours is an unshakable alliance...an alliance today that is stronger than ever," U.S. President Bill Clinton declares, and the United States and Korean presidents sit down at the

---

8. Edwin O. Reischauer Memorial Lectures, Harvard University, April 2, 1998.

White House together to confer.

Thus, from rather inauspicious beginnings, from some unusual "flotsam and jetsam" to a pageant of flags and flourishes, an influential partnership would emerge. But as close and effective as it has been, the South Korea-U.S. relationship has often been characterized by a high degree of asymmetry in the perceptions, objectives, capabilities, and influence of the two partners. Today, as we continue our look at the triangular relationship among the United States, China and Korea, we'll look below the surface on the Korea-U.S. side of this evolving triangle.

The Early Decades: A Slow Start[9]

The relationship was a cordial one when Korea and the United States signed a Treaty of Peace, Amity, Commerce, and Navigation in 1882. The Koreans looked to the United States for protection from the imperialistic ambitions of such countries as Japan and Russia, while the American envoys became close friends of Korea and defenders of Korean independence.

The year 1905 brought the first rift in relations, however, when to Korea's great disappointment, the United States acquiesced to Japan's domination of the peninsula. In return, through the Taft-Katsura memorandum, the U.S. gained Japan's acceptance of American domination of the Philippines.

For the next 40 years, until Korea was liberated in 1945, missionaries, educators and philanthropists were the only American presence in Korea. But these Americans contributed enormously in transmitting Western culture and education to Koreans, often arranging their study in the United States. And in their private capacity, they were for the most part also supportive of the Korean aspiration for independence.

During World War II, the United States was compelled again to confront the issue of Korean sovereignty at the Cairo Conference of December 1943, and the Yalta and Potsdam Conferences of February and July 1945. Lacking sufficient expertise and interest in the matter, however, the United States could draw only a vague outline of Korean independence, thus

---

9. Sung-Joo Han, *AFTER ONE HUNDRED YEARS: Continuity and Change in Korean-American Relations* (Seoul: Asiatic Research Center, Korea University, 1982), pp. 355–405.

mostly causing confusion and conflict in the discussions. As Professor Edwin O. Reischauer observed in a piece he co-authored for the *New York Times*: "The division of the peninsula was produced by external force applied largely through inadvertence...." Ultimately, the United States agreed to a divided occupation of Korea with the Soviet Union, an action which fuels blame from some for the country's division even today.

The first U.S. military contingents landed in Korea on September 8, 1945, as an occupying force and with the primary task of disarming the Japanese troops and maintaining order below the 38th parallel, a demarcation line hastily drawn by a couple of staff officers at the U.S. War and State Departments in the final hours of World War II. Over the next decade, the United States became the principal sponsor of the Republic of Korea, its protector from external military threats, and the provider of key economic assistance.

Post-Independence Relationship

Ever since the establishment of the South Korean government in 1948, its foremost foreign policy concern has been Korea's relationship with the United States. Eventually, the United States became the principal sponsor of the Republic of Korea, its protector from external military threats, and the provider of assistance for economic sustenance.

In the post-independence period, power and administration in Korea were highly centralized under Syngman Rhee, and this was particularly true in foreign policy. Furthermore, Korea's relationship with the United States constituted almost his entire foreign relations portfolio. For President Rhee, the ability to work with the Americans, if not direct experience in the United States, was a major criterion for appointing a person to a key position in government. His cabinets consistently reflected this preference, as Rhee felt comfortable with those who were educated in and familiar with the West, and United States, in particular. This was only natural, as Rhee had spent nearly four decades of his life in the United States as a student and an exiled nationalist.

Needless to say, Korea's heavy dependence upon the United States could not have materialized without an American willingness to lend assistance. And in fact, between 1948 and 1950, Syngman Rhee's pleas for U.S. involvement in Korea's security were largely ignored.

But after the outbreak of the Korean War, the situation changed drastically. Having made an enormous sacrifice in terms of lives and material, the United States could not accept a communist victory on the Korean peninsula without a serious loss of prestige and credibility; South Korea came to have a symbolic significance to the United States over and beyond its strategic value.

The United States saved it from a military takeover by Communist North Korea when the latter invaded South Korea in June, 1950. Soon after the Korean War, in which the United States suffered some 34,000 battle deaths and spent more than 18 billion dollars, the American and South Korean governments concluded a mutual defense treaty which has served as the formal basis of the alliance until today. Since 1953, the Republic of Korea has depended almost entirely upon the presence in Korea of U.S. troops and upon its air and naval protection to deter North Korea from launching another armed invasion.

The important role that the United States has played in the survival and development of South Korea in the post-Korean War period is indicated, at least in part, by the amount of economic and military assistance it provided for South Korea. During a 20-year period since the signing of the Mutual Security Treaty, the United States extended to South Korea nearly eight per cent of its worldwide foreign economic and military assistance. In fact, the United States has given South Korea more aid—a total of $11 billion by 1973—than to any other country with the exception of South Vietnam.

Thus a combination of many factors after the War—security considerations, anti-communist sentiment, protecting her investment in the Korean War, the American-Soviet rivalry, and the internationalist trend of U.S. foreign policy—provided a ready and permissive environment for the United States to establish a "protector" relationship with South Korea. The end result was that, in the latter half of this century, the United States replaced China of earlier times as the dominant influence on Korea, at least the southern half.

For Korea's part, President Rhee's chief foreign policy concerns in the post-War period consisted of the following three points: 1) the United States and its European allies were too "soft" on the communist threat throughout the world; 2) the U.S. did not fully realize the dangers of restoring Japan to major power status in Asia; and 3) American economic aid to Korea was insufficient in amount and inadequately administered. In addition, Rhee strove to keep the United States from interference in Korea's domestic political affairs.

Above all, President Rhee was fearful that the United States and its allies would grow tired of fighting in Korea and abandon their struggle, leaving South Korea vulnerable to another communist invasion. In 1953, when it became clear to Rhee that a truce was inevitable, he made his compliance with the prospective armistice contingent upon several conditions which included: 1) the United States must sign a defense pact with South Korea; 2) communist Chinese troops must be withdrawn from North Korea; and 3) the United States must provide economic and military assistance to South Korea. At the time, Rhee threatened that if the United States did not accept these conditions, it should allow South Korea to fight on alone.

Eventually, the United States had to dispatch to Korea several top officials, including Assistant Secretary of State Walter Robertson and Secretary of State John Foster Dulles, to persuade Rhee to accept the Armistice and refrain from obstructing it. Ultimately, the Rhee government was promised a bilateral security pact and a large scale aid program in return for abandoning demands for the withdrawal of the Chinese from North Korea and the immediate unification of the country.

Contrary to the widely accepted view that the security treaty was a concession to Rhee, the reality is that the U.S. probably would have concluded such a treaty with the Republic of Korea anyway. But it was significant that the envoys of the United States President came to him, asked for his cooperation in carrying out their policy, and then made it look like a concession to Rhee in order to lessen his opposition to the armistice.

Still, the Rhee government was unhappy about what is known as the "Monroe Doctrine formula" of the treaty under which, in the case of an armed attack on the other, each party would take an action "to be determined in accordance with its constitutional process." South Korea hoped, somewhat naively, that the United States would instead agree to a "NATO formula" with its automatic response provision.

President Rhee was reasonably successful in warding off what he resented as U.S. interference in Korea's domestic affairs. During the war, when President Rhee began to build up his dictatorial rule and alienate the Korean public, it appears that the United States was more preoccupied with the restoration of political stability. The U.S. feared that, if pushed too hard, Rhee might provoke incidents that would jeopardize its objectives of putting an early end to the war.

Even after the war, Rhee was considered to be the best hope for stability and order in Korea. And even if the American government had wished to bring about a change on the political scene, a premature intervention would only have resulted in entrenching President Rhee against the United States. It was only in 1960, when the Rhee government was ousted by a student uprising, that the United States abandoned its "long-suffering non-interference" as the *New York Times* put it. At that point, and then again toward the end of the Chun Doo-Hwan administration twenty-seven years later, U.S. involvement was critical to restoring democracy to South Korea.

On the whole, Syngman Rhee, despite his America-centered foreign policy and perhaps because of it, proved to be a tough bargainer as far as the United States was concerned. He persistently and loudly argued for a tough stand against the communists, for a stronger U.S. security commitment as well as more economic aid for Korea, and against the establishment of too close ties between the United States and Japan. As a result of his unyielding and often overly hawkish attitude, Rhee probably compromised much of his diplomatic effectiveness.

The election in 1948 of Syngman Rhee as the first president of the newly established Republic of Korea assured that it would seek close ties with the United States in its foreign policy. In post-World War II Korea, Rhee and other conservative nationalists had to wage a heated power struggle against the "left nationalists," as a result of which American help had been essential to them in the struggle even though U.S. enthusiasm for Rhee was not so great.¹⁰ Following Rhee's assumption of power, South Korea was immediately subjected to North Korea's political and military challenge. The Rhee government had only one place to turn to for help: The United States. Although the security requirements and economic needs of South Korea may by themselves explain South Korea's willingness to receive help from the United States, the extraordinary degree of South Korean dependence on the United States requires further explanation.

South Korean policy toward the United States was strongly affected by the fact that important positions within the Rhee government and his party were occupied by individuals who had close ties with the United States. For President Rhee, the ability to work with the Americans or having had experiences in the United States was a major criterion for appointing a person to a key position in government. He felt comfortable with those who were familiar with the West, and the United States in particular. A majority of Syngman Rhee's first cabinet, formed in August 1948, consisted of "Western-educated" individuals. In the 1950s, a relatively high proportion of the leaders of the Rhee government and the pro-Rhee Liberal Party had been educated in the West (mostly in the United States).¹¹ Despite the American government's rather unsympathetic attitude toward his nationalistic cause prior to 1945, Rhee remained a firm believer in the necessity of seeking American help in achieving Korea's independence before 1945, and economic development and security goals after 1948.¹² America was President Rhee's primary intellectual and psychological reference. As a result, Rhee was greatly responsible for the dependency that South Korea allowed itself to develop in its relations with the United States during the first 12 years of the Republic.

Another important point is that the Korean nationalist movement

---

10. Sung-joo Han, "Syngman Rhee: The Political Entrepreneurship of a Conservative Nationalist," *The Journal of Asiatic Studies*, Vol. 22, No. I (January 1979), pp. 97–103.
11. Kim Kyu-t'aek, *Han'guk chongch'i haengt'ae ron* [Korean Political Behavior] (Seoul, 1971), p. 177.
12. On this point, see Son Se-il, *Yi Sung-man gwa Kim Ku* [Syngman Rhee and Kim Kul (Seoul, 1970), esp. pp. 53–156.

had been directed against a non-Western country (Japan), thus making dependence on a Western nation less objectionable than it would have been had the country been colonized by a Western nation. On this point, Chong-sik Lee, a student of Korean nationalist movement, wrote: "The peculiar fact that Korea had become the colony of a non-Western power differentiates Korean nationalism from any other colonial nationalism. Whereas most of the colonial nationalists around the world looked upon the Western powers, or white race as a whole, with at best suspicion and at worst hatred, the Korean nationalists looked upon the Western world as the pioneer of liberalism and a new civilization."[13]

Also, it is often pointed out that Korea, having been a subordinate state to China during much of her history until the 19th century, came to develop a tradition or ideology of "serving the powerful country" (*sadae juui*), and that her twentieth-century leaders continued to exhibit traits which are derivable from such a "tradition."[14] It is not clear to what extent *sadae juui* was responsible for South Korea's highly dependent attitude toward the United States in the post-liberation period. It seems certain, however, that the tradition—to the extent that it was real—gave the dependence a certain degree of acceptability, not only among the leaders but also among the general public.

South Korean Relationship with the United States in the Post-Korean War Period

Since the Armistice in July, 1953, the South Korea government attempted to discourage U.S. efforts to reach an agreement with the Communists on convening a political conference which eventually met in the spring of 1954 in Geneva. South Korea initially refused to participate in the conference because it did not see the usefulness of negotiating with the Communists to begin with and particularly because of the inclusion of the Soviet Union in it. Once again, the United States had to bargain to get South Korean

---

13. Chong-sik Lee, *The Politics of the Korean Nationalism* (Berkeley, 1963), pp. 277–78.
14. Lee Ho-jae, *Han'guk oegyo chongch'aek ui isang gwa hyonshil* [The Ideals and Realities of Korean Foreign Policy] (Seoul, 1972), pp. 43–44.

cooperation. It promised to aid in strengthening the ROK army "greatly," and to see to it that American delegates in the conference would stand firm on the unification of Korea under a democratic government.[15] If the United States had failed to lead South Korea to the conference, it would have been blamed by the world for the failure of the Geneva Conference. Hence, it agreed to South Korea's new demands for increasing American responsibility for Korea's security.

The few months prior to the Armistice and the period preceding the collapse of the Geneva Conference marked the peak of Syngman Rhee's power as reflected in United States foreign policy. Rhee's power was negative in nature. It existed most effectively in times of crisis. His threats were most probably a means to wage his constant struggle to prevent the world from forgetting South Korean problems. As the immediate crises passed, such "power" would no longer play a major role in South Korea's relations with the United States.

Rhee also had great misgivings about what he considered was a "relaxation of tensions" policy that marked the Eisenhower presidency. He told the American public: "While we dream, hope, and plan for peace, the Communists talk and talk, distracting us from what they are doing behind the Iron Curtain. And what have they been doing? They have been building up the largest army in the world, the largest air force, the largest fleet of submarines, and developing their atomic and hydrogen bombs If we continue to sit still and ignore the enemy's acts because we want to believe his words, there probably will not be any war—or if there is, it will be a short one. But we will not like the outcome. To win a real peace in the world, we'll have to fight for it."[16] Even during the 1950s, Rhee's strongly cold-war rhetoric did not sit well among the American public who regarded his remarks as inflammatory and designed to involve the United States in dangerous confrontation with the Soviet Union for South Korean self-interest.

The counter-productive nature of Rhee's foreign policy behavior was

---

15. *New York Times*, April 24, 1954.
16. From President Rhee's CBS interview as cited in Robert T. Oliver, *Syngman Rhee and American Involvement in Korea, 1942–1960* (Seoul, 1978), pp. 470–71.

also evident in his handling of the "Japan question." In his view, the United States was making a mistake by strengthening Japan economically and militarily. Once again, Japan could become a dominant power in Asia and threaten not only the interests and security of her neighboring countries but also the United States as well. Furthermore, Rhee resented the fact that the United States appeared to support Japan in the dispute between Korea and Japan. Hence, Rhee cautioned the United States about its support of and ties with Japan. He also refused to negotiate diplomatic normalization with Japan unless Japan met his demands in areas ranging from reparation of property claims and fisheries question.[17] Thus the Korean President appeared to the American officials and public to be merely stubborn and obstructive at worst and anachronistic at best.

With regard to economic aid, Rhee considered U.S. aid quite inadequate for Korea's need after the war. At the same time, Rhee was dissatisfied with the arrangement under which the aid was administered directly by American officials. Between 1954 and 1960, Korea received more than $2 billion in U.S. economic aid. Although this was an amount far from being sufficient to reconstruct the war-devastated Korea, it did represent a large sum from the point of view of the Americans. It constituted more President Rhee was much more successful in warding off what might be considered as U.S. interference in Korea's domestic affair. Rhee was resentful of the growing concern of the United States over his undemocratic practices which increasingly alienated his government from the general public. It was during the war that President Rhee began to build up his dictatorial rule. Although the United States viewed the deterioration of democratic political structure in Korea with misgivings, it showed constraint in dealings with the Rhee government. In most cases, the United States went no further than issuing protests. During the war, it appears that the United States was most interested in an early restoration of political stability in Korea. It was preoccupied with the fear that, if pushed too hard, the President might provoke incidents that would jeopardize its objectives of putting an early end to the war. Even after the end of the war, Rhee was

---

17. *Ibid.*, pp. 465–70.

considered to be the best hope for stability and order in Korea. Even if the American government had wished to bring about a change in the Korean political scene, a premature interference by it would only have resulted in turning President Rhee further against the United States. The "incident" of Ambassador William Lacy is illustrative of this point.

When Lacy was transferred from the Philippines to Seoul in 1955 to serve as the U.S. Ambassador, Rhee had been informed in detail of how he had helped bring down Elpidio Quirino and install Ramon Magsaysay as President of the Philippines. President Rhee successfully maneuvered to have the U.S. State Department withdraw Ambassador Lacy from Seoul.[18]

It was only in 1960, when the Rhee government was ousted as a result of a student uprising, that the United States played an important role in the resignation of Syngman Rhee by abandoning its "long-suffering non-interference" as the *New York Times* put it.[19] It did so when conditions desired such an action and made it possible. But those conditions themselves were not and could not be created by the United States.

On the whole, Syngman Rhee, despite his America-centered foreign policy and perhaps because of it, proved to be a tough bargainer as far as the United States was concerned. He persistently and loudly argued for a tough stand against the Communists, for a stronger U.S. security commitment and more economic aid for Korea, and against the establishment of too close ties between the United States and Japan. As a result of the uncompromising and overly hawkish attitude, Rhee probably compromised much of his diplomatic effectiveness. The situation would change considerably after the collapse of his government in April 1960.

The American willingness to underwrite the financial requirements of South Korea's subsistence and defense was more than matched by the eagerness with which South Korea accepted the U.S. aid and depended on its help in wide-ranging areas from defense to economic development. The amount of economic aid that South Korea received from the United States during the 16-year period between 1954 and 1970 ($3.5 billion) was

---

18. *New York Times,* November 27.
19. *Ibid.,* May 1, 1960.

equivalent to nearly five per cent of South Korea's total gross national product for the same period. U.S. economic and military aid combined accounted for nearly one-tenth of South Korea's GNP in that period.

Aside from the enormousness and pervasiveness of U.S. role in Korea that the amounts of aid would indicate, one may state that the Korean armed forces owed their existence and functioning almost entirely to the United States. It gave military assistance in equipment, training, organization, and operational and tactical skills before, during, and after the Korean War.[20] Furthermore, ever since 1950, the Korean armed forces have been under the operational control of the United Nations Commander (a U.S. general), an arrangement that had resulted from an exchange of letters between President Syngman Rhee and General Douglas MacArthur in the wake of the Korean War.[21] The United States also assumed the burden of looking after the interests of South Korea in international organizations such as the United Nations where it acted, in the words of the U.S. government, as "the principal sponsor of the Republic of Korea as an applicant for membership."[22] It also spoke for South Korea in the Korean Armistice Commission meetings where the latter has been an observer.

Extremely close and generally cordial as it has been, the U.S.-South Korean relationship can, for the most part, be characterized by high degree of asymmetry in the perceptions, objectives, capabilities, and influence of the two partners. While the primary objective of the United States in entering into the relationship of alliance was to check the expansion of the Soviet and Chinese power in East Asia, South Korea's sole objective was to prevent another North Korean invasion and possibly to gain control of the northern half of Korea. While Korea, and even the Far East, represented only one segment of its worldwide concern to the United States, the world situation was important to South Korea only because of its relevance to its

---

20. On this point see Sung-joo Han, *The Failure of Democracy in South Korea* (Berkeley, 1974), pp. 46–54.
21. For the texts of the letters, Se-jin Kim, ed., *Documents on Korean-American Relations, 1943–7976* (Seoul, 1976), pp. 119–20.
22. *New York Times*, April 20, 1960.

own security.

South Korea-United States Relations in the 1960s

The United States and South Korea have thus carried on a one-directional, rather than mutual, relationship of assistance and influence. The United States, as already shown, has been the provider of help and, South Korea, only the recipient. The one-sided nature of the relationship has been also reflected in the relative influence of the allies. The United States has often unilaterally made major policy decisions that would have serious consequences for South Korea. It has also exerted considerable amounts of influence over South Korea's domestic and foreign policies as exampled by the role it played in the resignation of President Syngman Rhee in 1960, the establishment of a civilian government in 1963, the dispatch of Korean combat troops to Vietnam in 1965, and the cancellation by South Korea of a plan to purchase a nuclear fuel recycling plant from France in 1976.

Like most other countries, however, the Republic of Korea through its foreign policy seeks to advance the country's security, autonomy, prestige, and economic prosperity.[23] These goals often conflict with one another. It is a particularly poignant aspect of Korea's policy toward the United States that, while it has sought to maximize American help in achieving its security and economic progress, Korea at the same time has had to struggle to minimize the undesirable effects of the asymmetry that has pervaded its relationship with the United States.

In fact, U.S.-Korea relations have been undergoing changes in recent years. South Korea has shown a greater degree of willingness to attempt "self-reliance," not only in the economic and political arenas but also in national defense, while the United States is often too preoccupied with its own domestic and foreign problems to act like a full-fledged protector of South Korea. The changing relationship is the result partly of conscious policies of the two countries and partly of the changing international

---

23. K. J. Holsti, *International Politics: A Framework for Analysis* (Englewood Cliffs, 1972), pp. 130–53.

environment. Indeed, the U.S.-Korean relationship was strained in the 1970s by the failure of both countries to understand the underlying basis for the alliance and the structural changes of recent years. Korea failed to take account of the impact of Watergate and Vietnam on American policies and Asian policy. The United States did not fully recognize the passage of Korea from a client state to a more self-assertive nation.

However, that the alliance survived the simultaneous pressures during 1976–78 of troop withdrawal question, the so-called Koreagate scandal, and tensions over the issue of human rights is a testimony to the importance that the countries attach to their relationship and the strong interests that each country recognizes to exist in the alliance. In the following pages, this paper will review the record and changing nature of the U.S.-South Korean relationship and examine its present state as well as future prospects.

Bilateral Relations in the 1960s

Even after Syngman Rhee's departure from the Korean political scene, relationship with the United States remained the central concern of both the Chang Myon government (1960–61) and the military government that came to power as a result of coup d'état in May 1961. It was inevitable for both of them to seek U.S. support and approval which were indispensable not only national security and economic development but also for domestic and international legitimacy of the respective regimes. The two main diplomatic developments of significance for South Korea during the 1960s were, first, the diplomatic normalization between South Korea and Japan in 1965 and, second, the dispatch of South Korean combat troops to Vietnam in the second half of the decade.

Diplomatic normalization with Japan was sought by both the Chang Myon government and the government of President Park Chung-hee as a means of expanding Korea's foreign relations beyond relationship with the United States and of bringing pragmatism and realism into Korea's foreign policy. In this undertaking, the United States itself was instrumental. In the hope that friendship and cooperation between South Korea and Japan would lessen America's defense burden in East Asia, the United States encouraged the normalization talks while its representatives in Korea and Japan tried to persuade the two governments to come to terms with each other. Although the Korea-Japan diplomatic normalization, in fact, contributed significantly to a reduction of South Korean economic dependence on the United States, South Korea continued to remain totally dependent on the United States for its security. The South Korean dispatch of combat troops to Vietnam is a clear illustration of the point. It was also an event that would change the nature of Korea-U.S. relations significantly.

South Korea's participation in the Vietnam conflict, extensive and long-lasting as it was, can be understood and explained as a product of her alliance relationship with the United States. Korea sent troops to Vietnam, not as an ally of South Vietnam, but only as that of the United States. It is known that South Korea had a strong interest in preventing a communist victory and, hence, preventing American defeat in Indochina. But it was actually the declining credibility of U.S. power and the possible withdrawal of U.S. security commitments from Asia that Seoul viewed with the utmost concern, not necessarily the survival of the South Vietnamese state as such.

The foremost reason for South Korea's decision to send combat troops to Vietnam was to be found in its desire to prevent the weakening of the U.S. security commitment in Korea and, if possible, to further strengthen it. With the deepening of America's involvement in Indochina, doubts grew about the United States' security commitment and deterrence role.

U.S. military assistance to Korea was getting progressively smaller, down to $124 million in FY 1964 (1963–64), an all-time low since 1956. The average amount of annual U.S. military aid, which had been $232 million during the FY 1956–61 period dropped to $154 million for the FY 1962–65 period.[24] Advanced military equipment that had been promised to the armed forces was not forthcoming on schedule.[25] Most significantly, there were reports of U.S. plans, undoubtedly conveyed to the government through various channels, for a possible transfer to Vietnam of one or more divisions of U.S. troops from Korea in the event that additional troops from

---

24. The average amount of annual military aid increased to $367 million in the FY1966–1970 period (U.S. AID, *Overseas Loans and Grants*, 1974).

American allies were not available for combat.[26]

For this reason, a promise from the United States that it would not reduce its troop level in Korea was the major concession sought by the Seoul government during negotiations leading to the dispatch of the first Korean combat troops to Vietnam. Eventually, General Dwight E. Beach, the U.S. commander in Korea, and Ambassador Winthrop G. Brown jointly assured the government in a July 1965 letter that the U.S. "decision that there would be no reduction in U.S. force levels remained unchanged," and that "no U.S. troops would be withdrawn without prior consultation with the Republic of Korea."[27] As General Beach stated later, the Korean government interpreted this promise as a pledge that "no U.S. troops would be withdrawn without ROK approval."[28]

The South Korean government's position can be seen as that of trying to make the best of a difficult and unavoidable situation. Striving to gain as much financial benefit as possible was one way this was attempted. The government also succeeded in obtaining from the United States the long sought status-of-forces agreement covering U.S. military personnel in Korea. Most important of all, it used these circumstances as an opportunity to solidify America's security commitment.

The U.S. commitment underwent a substantial verbal upgrading in 1966 and 1967. During his visit to Korea in February 1966, Vice President Humphrey made the following statement, which was to be cited many

---

25. For example, Hawk I, a mobile, surface-to-air guided missile system, and Nike Hercules, a mobile or fixed site, surface-to-air or surface-to-surface guided missile system with nuclear warhead capability, had both been programmed for FY1963 but did not achieve operational status until 1965 and July 1966 respectively. See U.S. Senate, "United States Security Agreements and Commitments Abroad," Hearings Before the Committee on Foreign Relations, 91st Congress (Washington, 1971), p. 1651. The *New York Times* reported in 1966 the "speeding of U.S. arms to South Korea in return for the dispatch of a South Korean division to South Vietnam" (January 27, 1966).
26. Princeton N. Lyman, "Korea's Involvement in Vietnam," *ORBIS*, Summer 1968, p. 564.
27. Stanley Robert Larsen and James Lawton Collins. Jr., *Allied Participation in Vietnam* (Washington D.C.: Department of the Army, 1975), pp. 125–27.
28. *Ibid.*, p, 125.

times by other U.S. officials as a manifestation of the strongest possible commitment in Korea: "The United States government and the people of the United States have a firm commitment to the defense of Korea. As long as there is one American soldier on the line of the border, the demarcation line, the whole and the entire power of the United States of America is committed to the security and defense of Korea."[29]

President Johnson, during his November 1966 visit to Korea, "reaffirmed the readiness and determination of the United States to render prompt and effective assistance to defeat an armed attack against the Republic of Korea."[30] The phrase, "prompt and effective assistance," found in many subsequent U.S.-South Korean pronouncements together with Humphrey's above remark, was regarded by South Korea as a significant step in strengthening the U.S. commitment short of an actual revision of the defense treaty.[31]

Furthermore, the United States did not reduce its troop level in Korea until 1971, when about 20,000 men, or about one-third of the U.S. forces, were withdrawn.[32] Assurances that the existing U.S. troop level would be maintained were given not only by the U.S. commander in Korea and Ambassador Brown, as noted earlier, but by President Lyndon B. Johnson himself when he "assured President Park that the United States [had] no plan to reduce the present level of United States forces in Korea."[33] There is little doubt that the U.S. decision to maintain the existing troop level in Korea was directly related to the South Korean decision to dispatch combat troops to Vietnam.[34]

---

29. "United States Security Agreements and Commitments Abroad," p. 1725.
30. *Department of State Bulletin*, November 21, 1966, p. 778.
31. *Ibid.*, May 6, 1968, p. 576. For Korean reactions see "The Gifts of President Johnson's Visit to Korea," *Shin Dong-a*, December 1966, pp. 185–87.
32. *Department of State Bulletin*, June 4, 1973, p. 772.
33. *Ibid.*, November 21, 1966, p. 778.
34. Some would not agree with this observation. See, for example, Astri Suhrke, "Gratuity or Tyranny: The Korean Alliances," *World Politics*, July 1973, p. 520. Suhrke stated that "there was no apparent spillover effect [from Korea's Vietnam contribution] in other areas of inter-allied bargaining, such as the reduction of U.S. forces in South Korea."

The main effects of long-term significance for the U.S.-South Korean relationship included South Korea's success in achieving a greater degree of self-assertiveness vis-a-vis the United States and an expanded role in Asia's international politics. Until 1965, South Korea had been essentially an isolated, passive international entity depending almost exclusively on the United States for her international recognition and diplomatic activities. The situation began to change markedly after the arrival of the first South Korean combat troops in Vietnam.

Once South Korea became actively involved, it began to press on the United States its views on how the Vietnam conflict was to be resolved. Fearing possible U.S. "appeasement," the government urged the United States "to strive for a military victory" and "reject any peace that signified appeasement." It also sought a stronger voice in Vietnam policy-making among the allies, a role that top U.S. officials hastened to grant, at least in public statements.[35]

South Korea's increasing assertiveness toward the United States was most clearly shown in its refusal to send more troops to Vietnam despite repeated and urgent requests, initially made by President Johnson during his visit in November 1966, and repeated through Vietnam's Premier Nguyen Kao Ky in January 1967.[36] A special presidential mission consisting of General Maxwell D. Taylor and Clark Clifford also failed to persuade the South Korean government to increase its troop level in Vietnam.[37] It repeated its refusal in 1968. In the words of a news headline, South Korea began to "talk back" to the United States when it disagreed.[38]

One indication of Seoul's increased bargaining power vis-a-vis the United States was its extraordinary success in obtaining large sums of military aid during the years following the dispatch of combat troops to

---

35. See reports by the *New York Times* on Secretary of State Rusk's and UN Ambassador Arthur Goldberg's visits to Korea (July 9, 1966 and March 1, 1967).
36. *New York Times*, November 13, 1966; January 6, 1967.
37. *U.S. News and World Report*, January 12, 1970, p. 24; *New York Times*, August 4, 1967.
38. Bernard Krisher, "South Korea: The Courage to Talk Back," *Newsweek*, April 29, 1968, pp. 46–52.

Vietnam. Total U.S. military aid to Korea, which had been $815 million during a five-year period between FY 1961 and FY 1965 for an annual average of $336 million. In 1971, South Korea reluctantly accepted the U.S. plan to reduce its troop level in Korea from 63,000 to 43,000 only after securing a promise from Washington that it would support a five-year program to modernize the Korea armed forces at an estimated cost of $1.5 billion.[39]

Through its Vietnam experience, South Korea became exposed to America's weaknesses and aware of the limitations to her power. The South Korean contribution was almost indispensable to American efforts in Vietnam; the government was not only cognizant of this but also, on many occasions, tried to take maximum advantage of the situation. It often used the threat of withdrawing its troops as a major bargaining instrument. Doubts about America's military credibility became greater following the North Korean seizure of U.S. intelligence ship *Pueblo* in January 1968 and a U.S. response which the South Korean government considered inadequate. The U.S. failure to act forcefully in the Pueblo affair, and refusal to permit the South Korean army to strike back in retaliation for the North Korean assassination attempt on President Park in January 1968, raised questions about the United States' determination to repel aggression in Korea if it ever became necessary. The United States having lost its reputation for invincible power and will, the Korean government felt less intimidated than before in dealing with it.[40]

Another important factor behind South Korea's increasing assertiveness was the sense of self-confidence it acquired in the course of its involvement in Vietnam. Obviously, one major source of that confidence was its rapidly expanding economy, which grew by some 70 per cent during a five-year period between 1965 and 1970, the growth in part fueled by Vietnam-associated earnings. But South Korea also received a big psychological boost from its Vietnam experience. The initial South Korean military

---

39. *Department of State Bulletin*, March 1, 1971, p. 263.
40. "Soothing Seoul," *Time*, February 23, 1968. See, also, Townsend Hoopes, *The Limits of Intervention* (New York, 1969), p. 137.

operations were marked by remarkable successes and accomplishments, and military and political leaders were buoyed by the praise accorded Korean troops by U.S. military leaders.[41] In addition, the South Koreans remained tactically independent and administratively autonomous, with only the most general operational direction given them by the U.S. commander—a fact that contributed considerably to their sense of importance and independence. Having successfully resisted *de jure* operation control by the United States, the South Koreans now felt they had proven that they "could operate on their own without American forces or advisers looking over their shoulders."[42]

In the meantime, President Park's political position had become firmly established, a process the United States welcomed because of its desire for stable Korean leadership. Indeed, the situation had become such that Washington could have exerted little influence over the internal political balance even had it wished to do so. Economically, militarily and politically, the Park government was feeling increasingly confident in its relationship with the United States.

South Korea entered the Vietnam conflict with the primary purpose of preventing the withdrawal or weakening of the U.S. security commitment in Korea. After its entry, however, the government found itself striving for expanded objectives: i.e., exerting an influence on the Vietnam negotiations; increasing its international contacts and roles; acquiring greater bargaining power in its relationship with the United States; and maximizing economic gains. It was more successful in achieving the last two objectives than the first two. It was not able to exert much influence in the formulation of major U.S. policies, as seen in the 1969 declaration of the Nixon Doctrine or the signing of the 1973 Vietnam peace accord. The effectiveness of the Korean input was limited to how those basic policies were to be implemented once they were adopted.

---

41. See, for example, "Teaching Teacher," *Newsweek*, April 10, 1967; "Why Korean Troops Are So Effective in Vietnam," *U.S. News and World Report*, May 15, 1967; Larsen and Collins, Jr., *Allied Participation in Vietnam*, pp. 142–43.
42. *Ibid.*, pp. 135, 146.

Still, this represented a change in the alliance relationship between the United States and South Korea as it had prevailed up to 1965.[43] For such a change to come about, and for South Korea to be able to keep U.S. pressure on domestic matters at bay, required a combination of several factors, including: 1) the "stretching taut and thin" of American resources by the Vietnam involvement, which made South Korea's contribution invaluable to the United States; 2) South Korea's domestic political consolidation and success in economic expansion; and 3) a change in the international structure toward a lessening of bipolarity and the increasing importance of small states in world politics in general.

Korean Reaction to Carter Troop Withdrawal Plan

During the 1970s South Korea's primary concern was over the possibility of a significant reduction of U.S. military presence in Asia, particularly as a result of American setbacks in Vietnam. It feared that the 1971 withdrawal of 20,000 U.S. troops from Korea might be the beginning of a complete military pullout from Korea by the United States. South Korea tried to cope with the problem in three different ways: First, it sought to persuade the American policy-makers to maintain their military presence in Korea with pleas, publicity campaigns and reasoned arguments. Second, it made much effort in strengthening its own military capability through self-reliance as well as through foreign (American) assistance; and third, it tried to bring about a stabilization of the Korean situation through diplomatic means by initiating contacts and dialogue with the communist countries including North Korea, the Soviet Union and the People's Republic of China.

American advocates of U.S. troop withdrawal from Korea made the following arguments since the early 1970s: l) the United States should not maintain a position which might entail automatic involvement in a land

---

43. Even prior to this date, as described earlier, there had been a few exceptional instances in which South Korea was able to exert some influence on U.S. policymaking. See Chang Jin Park, "The Influence of Small States upon the Superpowers: United States-South Korean Relations as a Case Study, 1950–1953," *World Politics*, October 1975.

war in Asia; 2) South Korea no longer possessed sufficient strategic value for the U.S. ground troops to serve a "tripwire" function there; 3) since neither the Soviet Union nor China wished another war to break out in Korea, they would restrain North Korea from venturing an invasion; 4) the South Korean economy was becoming strong enough to provide its own security; 5) South Korea should free itself from a dependence syndrome and foster self-reliance and confidence; and 6) without maintaining ground troops in Korea, the United States would be able to support the ROK armed forces effectively if necessary in an armed conflict with air force and off-shore forces.

The South Korean government opposed American troop withdrawal plans on the following grounds: 1) since there was a serious military imbalance between North and South Korea, a premature withdrawal of the U.S. troops would tempt North Korea to try a military venture against the South; 2) the two Koreas would become involved in an expensive and dangerous arms race which might not rule out the development of nuclear capabilities; 3) as Japanese doubts about the credibility of U.S. security commitments to Asia increased, Japan would then either pursue rapid rearmament or accommodation with the Soviet Union; 4) the Soviet Union is engaged in an active military buildup in the Far East, and South Korea has an increasingly crucial strategic value to the United States, not only for the defense of Japan, but also for America's own security; 5) a unilateral disengagement by the United States would deprive it and the Republic of Korea of the opportunity to bargain with the communist side for the stabilization of the Korean situation; 6) the People's Republic of China, as well as most other countries in East and Southeast Asia, does not wish to see an early withdrawal of U.S. troops from Korea; and 7) a sudden disengagement from Korea by the United States would have a serious adverse effect on South Korea's continued economic growth, thereby depriving it of the opportunity to increase its military capabilities.

In order to make a forceful and effective representation of its view concerning America's security responsibility in Asia, the South Korean government felt a strong need to reach the American public and Congress directly. The result was a stepped-up effort to make their opinion and attitude more favorable to the Republic of Korea and to the causes it advocated.

Its main concern was to prevent the withdrawal of any more U.S. troops from Korea; in case this proved to be impossible, it hoped that the U.S. Congress would approve a generous support program for Korea's force improvement. The Korean government was also concerned about the adverse publicity in the United States given to Korean internal political and social situation. Subsequent public relations efforts of the South Korean government, a by-product of which was the so-called Koreagate scandal, in fact focused far more problems for Korean-American relations than it could have possibly contributed to solving.

The lobbying scandal, which dominated news headlines in both the United States and South Korea for nearly two years in 1977–79, significantly undermined the South Korean government's ability to conduct effective diplomacy. During that period, two parallel investigations, one by the U.S. Justice Department and the other by the House Committee on Standards and Official Conduct (the Ethics Committee) were conducted on allegation that, during the first half of the 1970s, South Korean agents had spent several million dollars to buy influence among U.S. Congressmen and other officials.[44] Although no official ties were conclusively established between the South Korean government and the lobbying activities of Park Tong-sun, considered to be the central figure in the scandal, its initial reluctance to comply with the requests of the U.S. investigators for the return of Park to the United States produced a serious strain in relations between the two countries. After months of negotiation, Park was allowed to return to the United States on a promise of immunity to be a witness in the "Koreagate" trials and to testify before the Congressional committees investigating the scandal. The thorny question of obtaining testimony from a former Korean ambassador to Washington was resolved by an agreement between the two countries under which the questioning of the ambassador was to be

---

44. A third probe, aimed primarily at exposing the activities of the Korean CIA in the United States, was conducted by the House Subcommittee on International Organizations headed by Representative Donald M. Fraser.

done in writing.

It was a testimony to the strength of U.S.-South Korean ties that, even during the height of the controversy between them over the scandal, relationship between the two countries remained basically cordial on the executive levels. Furthermore, no major legislation aimed at weakening American security commitments to Korea passed the Congress of the United States despite efforts to that effect by several legislators. In fact, it was precisely during this period that President Carter's troop withdrawal plan became to object of persistent attack from influential members of the U.S. Congress and military leaders.

President Carter's plan to withdraw all 33,000 American ground troops from Korea within a four to five-year period was announced at a press conference held on March 9, 1977, less than two months after his inauguration. Subsequently, the U.S. government disclosed that about 6,000 troops would be withdrawn by the end of 1978 in the first phase of the pullout plan. Although the withdrawal decision did not come as a complete surprise, the ROK government was disconcerted by the poor timing of the announcement. At the time, the U.S. Justice Department was broadening the scope of its investigation of the alleged Korean lobbying activities in Washington; the new American administration was also stressing the importance of the human rights question in its foreign policy. There was concern that the U.S. troop withdrawal decision would be construed as an American rebuke of the ROK government. It was also displeased by the fact that the United States had not sought assurances from the communist side to stabilize the Korean situation before taking unilateral action on troop withdrawal.

As it turned out, many American Congressional and military leaders had serious misgivings about President Carter's troop withdrawal plan. A February, 1978, report to the Senate Foreign Relations Committee by the late Senator Hubert Humphrey and Senator John Glenn was highly critical of the plan and called for legislation requiring President Carter to give Congress very detailed military justification before each increment of his planned withdrawal. In April, 1978, in a direct challenge to President Carter, the House Armed Services Committee voted overwhelmingly to prevent a premature withdrawal of American ground forces from Korea.

In response to a strong Congressional pressure, and in consideration of the evolving international situation in East Asia which involved the heavy military buildup in recent years by both the Soviet Union and North Korea, President Carter decided to postpone the withdrawal indefinitely after an initial pullout (in 1978) of some 3,500 troops. At the same time, U.S. air force strength in Korea was increased by some twenty per cent in manpower and number of aircraft in conjunction with the original ground troop reduction plan.

As a means of contributing to South Korea's force improvement program, the U.S. Congress approved in August, 1978, a $1.2 billion military assistance program for the Republic of Korea, including an $800 million military equipment transfer program. The South Korean air force also received additional F-4E Phantom jets from the United States in 1978–1979. Also planned was a $1.2 billion sale by the United States of 60 F-16 fighters to South Korea within the next few years. Moreover, the United States was said to have reiterated its readiness to support South Korea's defense industry.

It is difficult to determine the extent to which South Korea's "fire-fighting" diplomacy was responsible for President Carter's change of mind concerning the troop withdrawal plan and the U.S. government's continued concern about Korean security and support for its defense effort. In all likelihood, however, U.S. decisions concerning its security commitment in Korea—whether to withdraw troops or to postpone the withdrawal—were made independently of South Korea's diplomatic efforts aimed at influencing them.

President Nixon's visit to China in the spring of 1972 was responsible for the opening of the inter-Korean dialogue in July 1972. South Korean participation in the talks, probably encouraged by the United States, was aimed at exploring the possibility of ending the extreme hostility which prevailed in the peninsula for a quarter of a century. North Korea, by participating in them hoped to weaken America's justification for keeping troops in Korea and to secure a new respectability and status as a *bona fide* member of the international community.

Despite the fanfare and publicity which accompanied the initial round of meetings between the two sides, little progress was made in bringing the North and the South closer together. The first full conference of the South-North Korea Coordinating Committee opened in Seoul on November 30, 1972. The second conference was held in Pyongyang in mid-March, 1973 and the third in Seoul in mid-June, 1973. At the conferences, while the South advocated economic and cultural exchanges between the two areas prior to the settlement of political and military issues, the North insisted on a prompt peace treaty, the withdrawal of all U.S. forces from the South, and mutual troop reductions. A deadlock was inevitable. Each side feared that the other's proposal would weaken its own ideological, military and international positions. Thus, the dialogue remained stalled since the fall of 1973.

In the second half of the 1970s, South Korea was concerned that the United States might directly or through Japan establish some form of official relationship with North Korea without the reciprocal recognition of the Republic of Korea by the U.S.S.R. or China. As the North Korean government persistently explored possibilities of a direct contact with the United States, President Carter exchanged messages concerning such possibilities with North Korean President Kim Il Sung through such third parties as Marshall Tito of Yugoslavia, President Bongo of Gabon, and President Nicolai Ceausescu of Rumania. The Carter Administration publicly insisted, however, that talks with North Korea could take place only with the participation of the Republic of Korea.[45]

On the occasion of President Carter's visit to Korea in June, 1979, South Korea mounted a diplomatic offensive by issuing a joint declaration with the United States calling on North Korea to agree to hold a three-party conference of the United States, South and North Korea which would explore the possibility of reducing tension on the Korean peninsula. As North Korea adamantly rejected the offer, the South Korean fear of a possible direct contact between the United States and North Korea was

---

45. Interview with Richard Holbrooke, U.S. Assistant Secretary of State for East Asia and the Pacific, as reported in *Far Eastern Economic Review*, November 18, 1977.

allayed to a considerable extent.

Another significant development with regard to Korean-American relations in the 1960s and 1970s was the diversification of Korea's foreign economic relations. America's share in Korea's total trade dropped from 49 per cent in 1962 to 27 per cent in 1976.[46] By 1967, Japan overpassed the United States as the primary trading partner of South Korea, a position that Japan has maintained ever since. The combined share of the United States and Japan in Korea's total trade has been decreasing, from a high of 76 per cent in 1962 to 67 per cent in 1976.

The United States was still the largest creditor country with 35 per cent of South Korea's total loans as of 1976.[47] Since 1970, however, most of the loan has been coming from sources other than either the United States or Japan. In the "foreign direct investment" category, the United States lagged far behind Japan, by a ratio of three to one as of 1976. Since 1971, Japan's investment in Korea has been substantially higher than that of the United States. That Korea has been moving away from heavy economic dependence on the United States should be understood as both a cause and effect of its lessening dependence in overall relationship with America. In an apparent effort to reduce American resistance to the importation of Korea merchandise, particularly textile, shoes and electronic equipment such as color television sets, the South Korean government actively promoted purchase of American goods, particularly agricultural products and aircraft, for military as well as civilian use.

During the mid-1970s, South Korea was irritated by the ways in which the investigation of the alleged South Korean lobbying activities in the United States was handled by the U.S. government and press. More accustomed to a socio-political environment in which an organic relationship existed between various political entities such as the government and the press, it suspected that behind the investigation there might have been a coordinated and purposeful effort aimed at undermining its own prestige. As the United States was displeased by the apparent "audacity" to attempt

---

46. R.O.K. Economic Planning Board.
47. *Ibid.*

to influence the decision-making process in the United States, so was South Korea disappointed by the insensitivity of the United States to allow its junior alliance partner to be accused of wrongdoing by the mass media, legislature, and its own Justice Department.

A similar sentiment seemed to prevail within the South Korean leadership over the ways in which the "human rights" issue was being handled by the United States. Convinced that the United States security policy would not be substantially altered by those considerations alone, the South Korean government seemed to feel that Congressional hearings and other official pronouncements were intended more for embarrassing the Park government than to serve as a genuine policy-making process.[48]

The Korean-American relationship in the second half of the 1970s has exhibited strains and agonies of transition from what might be called a primarily patron-client relationship to some kind of a partnership even though the asymmetry between the partners in perceptions, power and influence remained. It is not hard to expect that the alliance which had been born and had functioned on the basis of extreme inequality between the partners, would experience a serious strain when there came a modification in that unequal relationship. The United States, while wanting on the one hand to disengage its ground troops from Asia and to minimize the possibility of getting involved in another Asian land war, still wished on the other hand to maintain its "managerial powers" concerning not only the military situation in the area but also internal arrangements of its alliance partner.

On the other hand, South Korea showed continued heavy reliance on the United States for not only its national defense but also in diplomatic and political support while at the same time resenting America's lingering

---

48. In 1974, the U.S. Congress approved a proposal to make a $20 million aid (in addition to the $145 million in military assistance approved without conditions) conditional upon South Korea's "making substantial progress in the observance of internationally recognized standards of human rights." See U.S. House of Representatives, "Human rights in South Korea and the Philippines: Implications for U.S. Policy," 94th Congress (Washington, D.C., 1974), p. 2. The South Korean government felt that this action was quite insulting.

paternalism and "interference." Furthermore, in its dealings with the United States, South Korea often showed a remarkable inability to understand the intricate workings of American political and policymaking process, often the result of projecting its own internal dynamics on the American scene.

In this connection, what Henry Kissinger had to say about the "troubled partnership" of the Atlantic Alliance in the mid-1960s seems quite appropriate to the Korean-American relationship: "Throughout much of the postwar period, the policy of our.... Allies has consisted essentially in influencing American decisions rather than developing conceptions of their own. This, in turn, produced querulousness and insecurity. At times, our Allies have seemed more eager to extract American reassurance than to encourage a consistent United States policy. Excessive suspicion has been coupled with formal pliancy.... This has led to a negativism characterized by a greater awareness of risks than of opportunities and a general fear of any departure from the status quo."[49] Nevertheless, steps were being taken to minimize problems of increasing the Korean share of defense burden and operational decision-making.

As an indication that the South Korean armed forces were expected to play an increasingly autonomous rule, for example, the U.S.-Korea Combined Forces Command (CFC) was officially activated in November, 1978. Designed to serve as an interim mechanism by which the operational control of the Korean armed forces would be eventually returned to the Koreans, the CFC arrangement in effect replaced the Taejon Agreement of 1950, under which then President Syngman Rhee had placed the entire ROK forces under the control of General Douglas MacArthur's United Nations Command. The new CFC structure enabled top South Korean military officers to participate in operational decision-making.

The 1970s was a period of not only transition in the U.S.-ROK relations but also of learning for South Korea. Gradually, more emphasis was given to persuading the American ally with reasoned arguments transmitted through official channel than emotional pleas or unorthodox methods.

---

49. Henry A. Kissinger, *The Troubled Partnership: A Re-Appraisal of the Atlantic Alliance* (New York: McGraw-Hill Book Co., 1965), pp. 6–7.

The conduct of policy toward the United States was being returned to professional diplomats and experts who had a greater familiarity with American political process and ways of thinking. At the same time, a serious reevaluation of South Korea's perennial dependence on the United States and America-centered foreign policy was being undertaken in view of the changed international circumstances. Thus, South Korea was making a serious effort to adjust its policy toward the United States as well as the policy-making and policy-executing mechanisms to the new requirements of the changed circumstances in the United States and in world politics.

Korea-U.S. Relations in the Post-Park Period

The death of South Korean President Park Chung-hee and the change of administration in both the United States and South Korea were followed by a drastic improvement in the relationship between the two countries. Thus, President Reagan's new ambassador to Korea, former professor of political science Richard L. Walker, declared on his arrival in Seoul in July, 1981, that relations between the United States and the Republic of Korea had "never been closer." Such a view is often expressed and is obviously shared, by many officials of both countries. They seem to believe that, with the coming of the Reagan administration, past "misunderstandings" between the two countries were effectively moved aside and a "new era" of amicability and cooperation has set in. Korean officials are particularly appreciative of the improved relationship as it came after many years of considerable difficulty and anxiety and at a time when there are signs of uneasiness in the U.S.-Japan relations. It also seems to have freed South Korea from its previous preoccupation with the bilateral issues with the United States, enabling its policy-makers to divert their diplomatic attention and energy to some of the other important areas, particularly Southeast Asia.

The new era of good feelings between the two countries which is claimed to have arrived presents several questions which require careful analysis. One question is to what extent the bilateral relationship has actually improved since the Reagan administration took office. Another question is whether the changed relationship is attributable exclusively to the Reagan administration's policy and attitude toward Korea and the

Korean problem that are different from the Carter administration's. A third question is what the political and diplomatic consequences the improved U.S.-South Korean relationship will have for the Korean peninsula and the East Asian region. Finally, one may ask how stable and enduring the rediscovered era of friendliness is likely to be. It is the purpose of this paper to offer tentative answers to these questions.

Korea and the Carter Administration

South Korea felt much anxiety during the Carter years because of the uneasy relationship with the United States. The strain in the bilateral relationship between the two countries was caused by a number of thorny issues including President Carter's plan to withdraw ground troops from Korea, the "Koreagate" scandal, controversy over human rights and democracy in South Korea, and South Korean relationship with North Korea. Underlying and aggravating the difficulty in the alliance were a major difference in strategic views concerning the Korean peninsula and what a senior U.S. diplomat called the "threats and demands approach" of the Carter administration.[50]

Generally speaking, U.S.-South Korean relations passed through three different phases during the Carter administration. Its first two years constituted the first phase when the relationship between the two countries sank to its lowest point. During this period, President Carter announced his troop withdrawal plan, the U.S. investigation of the Korean lobbying scandal was conducted in full steam, and the U.S. government assumed what South Korean officials described as a "hectoring" attitude concerning the human rights situation in Korea.[51]

During the second phase, which began toward the end of 1978 and lasted until the assassination of President Park Chung-hee in October, 1979, the Koreagate investigations came to an end, and President Jimmy Carter

---

50. Mike Mansfield, U.S. Ambassador to Japan, stated at a press conference on April 3 that the Reagan administration was formulating an Asian policy designed to avoid "threats and demands" (Associated Press, April, 3, 1981).
51. *Far Eastern Economic Review*, May 15, 1981, p. 44.

reversed his troop withdrawal decision. However, the U.S. government continued to express concern over the domestic political process in Korea. Relations were gradually being improved as the Carter administration moved closer to the South Korean view about the ever-present North Korean military threat to the south as well as about the strategic importance to the United States of the Korean peninsula. The United States seemed to be coming to the conclusion that it was better to live and work with the existing South Korean government which may be imperfect by its own political standard than jeopardizing its solvency and effectiveness thereby seriously risking the country's political, economic and social stability as well as security. Carter's eventual, if reluctant, "acceptance" of the Park government was clearly demonstrated by his visit to Korea in the summer of 1979.

The third phase of the Carter policy toward Korea began with the death of President Park in October, 1979. In the post-Park period, the United States was primarily concerned with South Korean security lest North Korea might be tempted to take a military advantage of the post-Park transition. Mindful of the authoritarian nature of the Park regime, however, the United States was also intent upon playing a key role in facilitating a smooth transition to a stable and competitive politics. However, the inflated expectations of full-blown democracy gave way to massive student demonstrations and social instability and the subsequent tightening of controls with a nationwide martial-law in May, 1980, followed by the consolidation of power by the military leaders headed by General Chun Doo-hwan. The Carter administration initially disapproved what it considered was a retrogression in the process toward democracy and then reconciled itself to accepting what appeared to be an inevitable development. Thus, toward the end of the Carter administration, the South Korea government felt comfortable enough with the Carter administration to the extent that its leaders were not excessively worried about Carter's possible victory in the November, 1980, presidential election.

One can argue, therefore, that the Reagan administration took office to bring to a rapid fruition a policy—and process which had been started already, if belatedly, by the Carter administration toward the end of its term. It was a policy intended to restore mutual understanding, cooperation and trust between the two governments. To point this out is not to underestimate the seriousness of the difficulties the relationship between the two countries after Carter took office or to ignore the persistence of certain degree of strain between the two governments. The strained nature of the bilateral relationship during the Carter period was partly the making of President Carter's own foreign policy. But to a significant part, it was also the result of circumstances that were not his administration's own making.

The revelations concerning Korean lobbying activities came at a time when, in the aftermath of the Watergate and Vietnam experiences, the American public was in a strong mood to expose and chastise any impropriety by the officials of either their own government or of another country. In the face of this trend in public attitude and ideological swing toward the left, it would have been difficult for any U.S. government, even a conservative one, to defy the public pressure to conduct a thorough investigation of what appeared to be a major scandal involving a foreign country.

On its own part, the Carter administration came in with a campaign promise of troop withdrawal that proved to be unrealistic and with an inadequate understanding of the strategic and political issues involving Korea. Its strategic premises on which the troop withdrawal plan was based were shaken by the disclosure of heavy military buildup undertaken during the 1970s by both North Korea and the Soviet Union. They were strongly challenged by many American Congressional and military leaders who had serious misgivings about the troop withdrawal plan.

Although President Carter eventually abandoned the plan by deciding in the spring of 1979 to "hold in abeyance" any further withdrawal of combat troops from Korea, the damage had been done as mistrust and disappointment pervaded in the traditionally cordial relationship between the two allies which had fought together in the Korean War and the Vietnam conflict.

Throughout the four-year period, the Carter administration, perhaps in its eagerness to justify its troop withdrawal policy, applied pressure on the South Korean government to reopen communication and seek accommodation with North Korea which remained adamantly hostile to South Korea since the breaking up of the South-North Korean dialogue in 1973. During his visit to Seoul in 1979, President Carter is said to have induced the unenthusiastic Park government to join the United States in proposing a tripartite talk among the United States and the two Koreas. The South Korean government was also constantly on alert lest the United States should unilaterally establish some kind of an official relationship with North Korea.

The main source of strain between the two countries which persisted toward the end of the Carter administration, however, was what the South Korean government considered to be unwarranted interference in Korea's internal affairs done in the name of human rights and democracy. The Carter administration did not seem to have recognized, or taken into consideration, the limited nature of U.S. leverage in Korean domestic political process. To be sure, the United States still enjoyed a considerable degree of influence and prestige among the political circles in South Korea. But this influence could not translate into power as it existed in a diffuse rather than goal-specific way. The United States did and could make itself felt in the South Korean political process but not necessarily in a way that enabled it to achieve a specific goal, and certainly not in matters to which the South Korean authorities in power attached vital political importance.[52]

The Carter administration was a captive of its own rhetoric and style of promoting human rights in other countries even when its method was proving to be counter-productive for the cause it stood for. In dealing with a government it found disagreeable, the United States could either attempt

---

52. Even though the United States, through the UNCommand, still held the operational control of the Korean armed forces as of 1980, it was not in a position to prevent (even if it wanted to) the movement of Korean troops by the Korean commanders unless the United States could establish clearly that such a movement had a direct bearing upon South Korean security. Furthermore, the United States discovered that it had no realistic recourse once defiance of the R.O.K.-U.S. agreement on mobilization of troops was made a *fait accompli*.

to weaken it or embrace it, and use its political influence accordingly. The problems with the first "option" were obvious. It could only result in antagonizing the existing regime without necessarily weakening or removing it. Even if the United States succeeded in doing so, there was no guarantee that it would not result in an even more undesirable political situation as happened in Iran.

The second option would have required some degree of consensus in the United States that the first was not a realistic alternative and the conviction of the U.S. administration that the encouragement of tolerance and discouragement of excesses had to be done in the most discreet way. One problem with following such a course was the possibility of the criticism that the United States was supporting an undemocratic government. In the event, the Carter administration followed neither of the two courses in Korea, but chose instead a middle course of making open criticism and giving warnings only to irritate the Park government. "Sanctions" were applied but were rarely effectual. They were actually not meant to be except as a gesture of displeasure or concern. The result was a greater degree of mistrust, defensiveness and inflexibility on the part of the Korean government without making it any easier for the U.S. government to provide South Korea with the needed support in the security area.

This is not to argue that the Carter administration's human rights policy as it applied to Korea was without any positive consequences. Although the Carter administration itself achieved little more than consciousness-raising, in an ironic way, its human rights policy through the unsuccessful record made it easier for the successor administration to do things differently.[53] The Reagan administration inherited a situation which was far more congenial to its conservative predilections than it would have had four years earlier. It took full advantage of President

---

53. According to Stanley Hoffmann, one merit of the Carter administration was "its determination to cope with major, long-term problems including human rights." He observed: "In some instances, little more. was achieved than consciousness-raising. In others, partial victories were won." See Stanley Hoffmann, "Requiem," *Foreign Policy*, Spring 1981, p. 6.

Carter's difficulties in his Korea policy. Without the unsuccessful experience of the previous administration, it would have been difficult for President Reagan to reverse its policy and adopt one of embracing and supporting the Chun government in Korea.

The Reagan Administration's Korea Policy

President-elect Reagan's decision to invite South Korean President Chun Doo-hwan to Washington had an element of risk as well as opportunity. The negotiations leading to President Chun's trip, which carefully bypassed the State Department and the regular diplomatic channels, were conducted for almost two months prior to its announcement on President Reagan's inauguration day. Thus, there was a good possibility of premature disclosure with potentially very embarrassing consequences for the president-elect. He was also placing his honeymoon with the Congress and the public on the line considering the possibility that domestic political evolution might stall in Korea or Mr. Chun could encounter a hostile reception in the United States. Above all, Mr. Reagan had to have the faith that the Kim Dae-jung issue would be resolved in a satisfactory way and that he would get the credit for it. There can be no doubt that Reagan and his advisors knew President Chun's Washington visit was to take place *before* his election for a seven-year term under the newly adopted constitution.[54]

By his decision to invite Chun to Washington, Reagan accomplished what his predecessor could not with protests and warnings. He gave the Korean government assurance of support and thus a greater degree of self-confidence and sense of autonomy. He thus succeeded in making the South Korean government more flexible. Furthermore, in one bold stroke, Reagan put the world on notice that his administration intended to

---

54. The Reagan team was not insensitive to the charge that its presumed indifference to the human rights question might nullify whatever success the Carter administration had on that issue. Thus, only two weeks after his election, Reagan felt it necessary to warn through his aide (presumably Richard Allen) against the carrying out by the ROK government of Kim Dae-jung's death sentence (*New York Times*, November 19, 1980).

practice what he had been preaching—placing security and loyalty ahead of other considerations (including human rights).

Reagan's basic strategic objective in Asia, as it became clearer after he assumed the presidency, was the ending of what he considered as a decade of retreat and vacillation by the United States. In order to "check Soviet expansionism in the region and restore American leadership," he was hoping to build a loose grouping of friendly powers with Korea as the key element in the scheme. Thus, he made no secret of the fact that the U.S. military posture in Asia in general and in Korea in particular would be strengthened rather than weakened and that the United States would not be niggardly in supporting South Korean forces improvement program. Particularly gratifying to the Korean leaders was the fact that for Reagan and his aides the Cold War has not yet faded away and that they recognized the strategic value of the Korean peninsula for its own sake rather than as an outpost for the defense of Japan, an impression often conveyed by the policies of the previous U.S. administrations.

The Chun-Reagan meeting, which took place at the White House on February 2nd, "glowed with warmth and fresh confirmation of America's defense commitment to South Korea."[55] It produced a joint communique in which President Reagan assured that "the United States has no plans to withdraw U.S. ground combat forces from the Korean peninsula," while confirming that it would "make available for sale to Korea appropriate. weapons systems and defense industry technology necessary for enhancing Korea's capabilities to deter aggression."[56] The communique also promised the immediate resumption of a series of government-level consultations, some of which had been stalled by the Carter administration over human rights and other domestic political questions.

President Chun and those who accompanied him to the United States were elated with the results of the visit which far exceeded expectations. They were pleased and gratified by the warm reception they received not only from the members of the Reagan administration but also from those

---

55. *Far Eastern Economic Review*, May 15, 1981, p. 44.
56. *Korea Herald*, February 3, 1981.

of the Congress and the Democratic Party. Upon his return to Korea on February 7, Chun declared that the main result of the visit was "the restoration of trust," implying that it had been missing during the previous years.[57]

More immediately, the visit represented a decisive political boost to Chun, who was up for a seven-year term presidential election scheduled for February 11th. Reagan's invitation gave Chun the opportunity to demonstrate that he had the caliber of a statesman and to outdistance his other military colleagues in prestige and stature. All these, coupled with Chun's complete electoral victory, contributed to making his government more self-confident and flexible as well as less sensitive about the appearance of U.S. involvement in Korean politics.

Evidence of closer ties between South Korea and the United States could be found in the ensuing months in a number of areas. First of all, the United States has expanded its security support for Korea. Strengthening defense posture in Korea is being sought through two related ways: augmentation of U.S. forces in Korea and active assistance of Korean military modernization programs. As publicly announced by General John A. Wickham, Jr., commander of the U.S.-Korea Combined Forces Command, the "combat readiness" of the U.S. forces is being improved in many ways including the replacement of F-4 aircraft with the F-16 fighters and deployment of a U.S. Air Force A-IO close air support squadron over the next two years.[58]

In late April, at the U.S.-ROK security consultative meeting held in San Francisco, Secretary of Defense Caspar Weinberger unequivocally confirmed that "the United States nuclear umbrella will continue to provide additional security to the Republic of Korea."[59] The joint statement of the defense ministers of the two countries issued at the end of the San

---

57. *Ibid.*, February 8, 1981.
58. The Pentagon revealed in early July that the first U.S. Air Force F-16 fighters to be based overseas had arrived in Korea to join the 8th Tactical Fighter Wing (*Korea Herald*, July 9, 1981).
59. *Ibid.*, May 1, 1981.

Francisco meeting contained probably the strongest expression of U.S. security commitment in Korea made in almost fifteen years. Saying that the security of Korea was "pivotal" to the peace and stability of Northeast Asia and its own security, the United States reaffirmed to render "prompt and effective assistance to repel aggression against the Republic of Korea."[60]

It is equally significant that the United States gave the assurance that it would provide "a wide range of support, including appropriate sophisticated technology, the sale of equipment, and improved Foreign Military Sales credits for the enhancement of the defense of the Republic of Korea."[61] In this connection, the U.S. Congress approved in late May the sale of 36 F-16 fighters to Korea which the Reagan administration decided to deliver over the period of three years, starting in 1983. In addition, the United States began to deliver F-5 jet fighter "parts" for aircraft manufacturing in Korea and transferred a 4500-ton destroyer. The highly visible arms transfer activities by the United States are being conducted as a part of its overall global arms sales policy, a distinctive aspect of which was to "sell arms to friendly countries without inspecting their human rights policy too closely."[62]

The Reagan policy concerning arms sale to Korea was obviously intended to give notice to North Korea and the Soviet Union about firm U.S. commitment to South Korean security and to demonstrate its faith in and support for the Chun government. At the same time, it was intended to put pressure on Japan and other "allies" of the United States to do more for the regional defense. Needless to say, South Korea is satisfied with the new security policy of the Reagan administration while it has put Japan in a somewhat uncomfortable position.

Although the ruling LDP government recognizes the increasing Soviet military threat in Northeast Asia and accepts the U.S. view that something

---

60. *Ibid.*
61. *Ibid.*
62. Associated Press, July 11, 1981. It is also believed that, under the Reagan administration, terms of the FMS credits have been substantially improved to facilitate the South Korean procurement of U.S. arms.

has to be done to counterbalance the Soviet military buildup, it has shown reluctance, largely for domestic political reasons, to fully cooperate with the United States in taking strong measures for regional security in general and South Korean security in particular. It is also concerned that a rapid and open military buildup in and around South Korea might provoke the Soviet Union and North Korea into taking countermeasures which might in turn trigger a new round of arms race in the area. The issue of more immediate concern for Japan is, however, how to cope with the pressure of the Reagan administration on Japan to make a greater contribution to the security of the Northeast Asian region as well as of Korea.

In effect, the Reagan administration has openly taken the side of Korea in the traditional disagreement between Korea and Japan concerning the nature of security threat in Korea and the desirable degree of Japanese contribution to Korean security. Top Japanese officials who visited the United States, including Prime Minister Suzuki and Defense Agency Director Omura, were reminded of the "vital" nature of Korea for the security of Asia, and were reportedly urged to make a greater financial contribution (perhaps in the form of economic cooperation) as an indirect way of assisting Korean security efforts. The United States asks Japan to substantially reinforce her naval and air forces of the Self-Defense Forces to implement effective measures in case of an emergency in East Asia involving the Korean peninsula. The U.S. requests include the assurance of Japanese mobilization of rear area support for a possible war in Korea.[63]

U.S. support of the Korean position has 'emboldened the South Korean government to seek a reported amount of ten billion dollars or more in yen-denominated official loans and Export-Import Bank credits to be furnished over five years as Japanese capital cooperation in Korea's fifth five-year development program starting in 1982. The central Korean argument in support of the request is supposed to be that it is proper for Japan to increase its economic aid to Korea because of Japanese security benefits from Korea's defense efforts. It is unlikely that, under the present Japanese domestic political circumstances, the Korean government with the support

---

63. *Asahi Shimbun*, June 12, 1981.

of the Reagan administration will succeed in persuading Japan to make as much contribution to Korean security as it hopes to obtain. However, Japan may find it necessary to take a more cooperative stance to the United States as there is growing apprehension that U.S.-Korean ties might outpace her own relationship with the United States.

Strengthened ties with the United States have also had a significant bearing on Korean relationships with other countries. Korea now seems to take a much more relaxed and flexible attitude toward Japan as she is convinced that the United States no more judges its security interest in Korea through the "Japanese prism" as it sometimes seemed to be the case in the past. It is also likely that the Reagan administration is making a somewhat greater effort in South Korea's behalf for the improvement of relationship between Korea and China.

At the same time, improved relations with the United States have enabled Korea to pay greater diplomatic attention to countries other than the United States. President Chun's highly publicized trip to the ASEAN countries in June and July can be understood in this light. The fact that South Korean foreign relations have become increasingly active and productive since the Reagan administration took office is an indication of the crucial nature of South Korean relationship with the United States. In an ironic way, the United States, by maintaining close and cooperative relationship with South Korea, has enabled it to expand and diversify its diplomatic activities.

In the economic arena, the Reagan administration has also given the impression that it is more sympathetic to South Korean interests than the previous administration. It has stopped the occasional practice of directing U.S. representatives in international financial organizations such as the World Bank and the Asian Development Bank to abstain in votes on Korean projects to show U.S. displeasure over political developments in Korea. In addition, it has refrained from objecting to the termination of shoe quota on products from Korea and Taiwan; it has also increased the Korean quota of fishing in the U.S. waters.

These decisions may not be directly related to the Reagan administration's Korea policy as such. It is quite probable that a Democratic administration (if Carter had been reelected) would have done the same thing. The lifting of shoe quota would benefit Taiwan more than South Korea. The measures might have been intended primarily to arrest domestic inflation in the United States. Expansion of the fishing quota benefited other countries (including the United States) as well as Korea. The important thing here is the perception of the Korean officials that such "favors" are directly related to President Chun's visit to the United States and the Reagan administration's sympathetic policy toward Korea. Indeed, many of the measures taken by the United States, economic and otherwise, appear to fit quite nicely to the Reagan policy intended to "reward friends."

The North Korea Question

It is impossible to think of a U.S. policy toward South Korea except with reference to the existence of a hostile North Korea and the presence of its military threat to the south. Not surprisingly, North Korea welcomed President Carter's announcement in March 1977 of his decision to withdraw U.S. ground troops from Korea. But it did not take the Pyongyang government long to realize that the withdrawal would be accompanied by an extensive South Korean force improvement program as well as the augmentation of the U.S. air force contingents which, it was announced, would remain in Korea indefinitely.

In any case, the withdrawal plan itself was eventually reversed by the Carter administration. Furthermore, the Carter administration did not respond positively to North Korea's long-standing offer, occasionally renewed, for bilateral negotiations on a peace treaty. The United States insisted instead that it would not negotiate with North Korea unless South Korea participated. North Korea was very disappointed by the Carter administration for its failure to go through with its troop withdrawal plan and by the U.S. refusal to negotiate directly with North Korea.

At the same time, the Carter administration also caused South Korean anxiety by trying to persuade it to reopen dialogue with North Korea which had been deadlocked since 1973. The South Korean government felt that the Carter administration was eager to achieve a political solution of the Korean question even at the risk of sacrificing South Korean interest. In this connection, it was also concerned about the possibility that the United States might establish some kind of a direct contact with North Korea against South Korean wishes. In 1979, a U.S. table tennis team and a number of U.S. newsmen visited North Korea. It seemed that North Korea's quest for increased contact with the United States was making some headway in 1980 when Congressman Stephen Solarz and former State Department official Tom Reston traveled to North Korea in a private capacity (on separate occasions). Congressman Solarz's well-publicized trip included a meeting with North Korean President Kim Il Sung.[64]

In all probability, their North Korean visits were made without the encouragement or endorsement of the State Department. However, the South Korean government remained unhappy that the Carter administration failed to stop them from making the trip. Thus, the Carter administration alienated and disappointed both the South and North Korean governments with its seemingly inconsistent policy toward the two Koreas.

By contrast, the Reagan administration has shown an unequivocal attitude toward North Korea and the inter-Korea relations. Soon after taking office, the Reagan administration disavowed the Carter-Park proposal of June 1979 for a tripartite conference among the United States and the two Koreas. Thus, Secretary of State Haig stated on January 30 that he had not proposed any three-way talks and that he did "not anticipate any until there has been a very thorough review of the desirability of such talks."[65] Instead, the United States strongly endorsed President Chun's proposal of January 12th and June 5th for a direct, personal meeting between the South and North Korean leaders. Furthermore, at every opportunity, top U.S. officials (in many cases military officers) have called attention to the heavy North Korean military buildup in recent years and emphasized the seriousness of North Korean military threat against the South.

In the Reagan-Chun communique, the United States made it clear that South Korea must be a full participant in any U.S. negotiations with North

---

64. Young C. Kim, "North Korea in 1980: The Son Also Rises," *Asian Survey*, January 1981, pp. 120–21.
65. *Korea Herald*, January 30, 1981.

Korea and that the United States would not take any steps toward establishing an official relationship with North Korea unless they are reciprocated toward South Korea by North Korea's "principal allies" (the PRC and the Soviet Union). In March, the Reagan administration turned down the request of North Korean observers at the United Nations to travel outside of New York, presumably because of the "extraordinary level of crude invective being hurled at the U.S. and President Reagan personally by the North Korean government."[66]

Because of the Reagan administration's firm and unequivocal policy toward North Korea, the South Korean government seems to feel somewhat less concerned about private U.S. citizens visiting North Korea. It should be also pointed out that, in the United States, there is the view that, since there is less danger of causing South Korean apprehensions about the Reagan administration's sincerity on the North-South Korean issue, private visits to North Korea can and should be encouraged. However, the South Korean authorities will begin to feel uneasy again as the number of U.S. visitors to North Korea increases.

The Reagan administration does not hesitate to emphasize that the emerging relationship between the United States and the People's Republic of China will have positive impact on Korea. For example, General Wickham, who seems to make more frequent policy statements under the Reagan administration than before, openly stated the view that "your [Korean] interests are well served by the growing relationship that we [the United States] are developing with China."[67] On the other hand, the United States is concerned that the Soviet Union may be spurred to support North Korea's aggressive policy and its military buildup efforts.

The Soviet Union may wish to play a disruptive role in Korea in order to bring North Korea closer to the Soviet side and as a way of counteracting the developing cooperative relationships among the United States, Japan and the PRC. For the moment, however, the Reagan administration seems to judge that the Soviet Union is not likely to support the North Korean

---

66. *Ibid.*, March 17, 1981.
67. *Ibid.*, July 24, 1981.

aggression as long as the United States maintains a strong military presence on the Korean peninsula.

In substance, President Reagan's North Korea policy does not represent a drastic departure from President Carter's. The main difference can be found in the style. The former shows more straightforwardness and forcefulness in pursuing a very similar policy that the Carter administration had toward the end of its term. South Korea feels that the Reagan administration is more dependable and more readily willing to accept the South Korean view of North Korean threat and the way to deal with it.

Future Perspective

Former Assistant Secretary of State for East Asia and Pacific Affairs Richard Holbrooke, who had been closely involved with the Carter administration's Korea policy stated recently that the present relations between Korea and the United States are "in the best shape" in 10 years and that "such best relations between the two allies have not come from the change of the U.S. administration but from the positive efforts of the Korean government."[68] Although the statement gives too little credit to the Reagan administration, it does underscore the fact that there is a high degree of continuity in the Korea policy of the Carter administration during its later period and that of its successor.

It seemed apparent that the Carter administration was moving toward "embracing" the Chun government in Korea. In August, 1980, General Wickham conditionally endorsed General Chun as Korea's new president in a press interview with the *Los Angeles Times*. The interview was disavowed by both the State and Defense departments, but there was no indication that General Wickham was reprimanded in any way for his highly political statement.[69] Vice President Walter Mondale was indicating before the U.S. presidential election in November 1980 that there would be a summit meeting between Carter and Chun if Carter were to be reelected.[70]

---

68. *Ibid.*, July 14, 1981
69. *New York Times*, August 13, 1980.
70. *Korea Times*, October 5, 1980.

One may argue, therefore, that the main difference between the two administrations in their Korea policy is that, while the evolving circumstances within and outside of Korea toward the end of President Carter's term *forced* the reluctant President to adopt a set of policies which seemed to be inconsistent with his earlier policy commitments, the same circumstances have *permitted* President Reagan to follow a similar set of policies which are consistent with his own ideological orientations and style. By the second half of 1980, the following points became fairly clear to the United States (both to the Democrats and the Republicans): that President Carter's earlier policy of reducing U.S. military presence in Korea had to be reversed, particularly in light of the extensive military buildup by North Korea and the Soviet Union; that there were severe limits to what the United States could accomplish with its policy of actively promoting human rights in other countries; and that the restoration of trust and friendship with the Korean government leaders was an important step toward reestablishing U.S. presence and leadership in East Asia. The Reagan administration thus made the most of the given circumstances which allowed it to pursue the kind of Korea policy that it would have felt most comfortable with in any case.

The above review of U.S. policy toward Korea during the past several years should not convey the impression that there are no remaining or new problems in the U.S.-South Korean relations. It is quite possible that the officials of both countries have become overconfident and complacent about the bilateral relations between the United States and South Korea because of their recent successes in improving them. It would make them underestimate divergence of attitudes and exaggerate convergence of interests. The Korean officials in particular tend to construe wishful thinking as reality for both psychological and political reasons.

But the reality is not as trouble-free as one might wish it to be. Public opinion surveys in the United States show that Korea is not one of the favorite countries among the American people.[71] Conflict of interests in the economic sphere, particularly in connection with trade restrictions, will remain and probably grow.[72] Korean economic activities in other continents will not always coincide with American diplomatic objectives.

Korea will continue to be sensitive to the possibility of foreign "meddling" in domestic affairs. Thus, sources of potential conflict and tension remain despite the appearance of drastic improvement in U.S.-Korean relationship under the Reagan administration. On the whole, however, the American-Korean alliance is thriving, at least for the time being.[73]

Conclusion

The preceding review of South Korean-U.S. relations since the end of World War II indicates that there are elements of both change and continuity in the nature of their bilateral relationship. Generally speaking, however, friendly ties and strongly felt sense of common interests have survived change of governments in the two countries and power realignment in world and regional relations.

Throughout the entire life-span of the Republic of Korea, security concerns were central to its foreign policy and particularly to Korean-American relations. Only the United States was capable of and willing to provide South Korea with the assurance and assistance necessary for its security and defense. Furthermore, South Korea desperately needed American help for its economic sustenance and development, at least well into the 1960s. Hence, the United States loomed so large in South Korea's overall foreign relations that it could hardly give serious attention to other

---

71. A 1980 survey by the Potomac Associates which measured "levels of like and dislike" discovered that, in "favorable" ranking, South Korea was behind such countries as the Philippines, China, Saudi Arabia, Taiwan, Singapore, India and Thailand. See William Watts, "Americans Look at Asia: A Need for Understanding," mimeo., Washington, D.C., 1980, p. 4.
72. According to ROK government data, Korea is at present the 10th largest market for the United States, and the second largest importing nation in Asia after Japan. In 1980, Korea's imports from the United States reached $4.9 billion or 21.9% of her total imports. Korean exports to the United States amounted to $4.6 billion or 26.3% of total exports in the same year.
73. The state of the U.S.-South Korean relationship as of August, 1981, is a far cry from what it had been a year before. See Sung-joo Han, "South Korea and the United States: The Alliance Survives," *Asian Survey*, November 1980, pp. 1075–1086.

regions or countries until recently.

Although the United States still does, and will continue to, play a central role in South Korea's security for the foreseeable future, there have been taking place certain changes in international and national conditions that both enable and require the Republic of Korea to break out of the preoccupation with the United States in its foreign policy.

The most important change has been a realignment among the major powers in East Asia resulting from the development of cooperative relationships between the People's Republic of China on the one hand and the United States and Japan on the other. It has given South Korea an opportunity to seek an official contact with the PRC and the expectation that the latter might succeed in persuading the North Korean government to accept a formula under which the two Koreas can be "cross-recognized" by the major powers. The Soviet Union, it is hoped by South Korea, would attempt to counter the PRC's anti-Soviet encirclement campaign in Asia by stretching a conciliatory hand to the Republic of Korea. The mere process of working toward the end of stabilizing the Korean situation has given South Korea an opportunity to broaden its international perspective and arena of activity and involvement.

Another important change has been South Korea's rapid and remarkable economic growth and expansion which has compelled it to look far beyond the United States as well as Japan for economic exchange and cooperation. It has now expanded its horizon to such remote areas as the Middle East, Southeast Asia, Western Europe, South America and Africa. In those places, it seeks export opportunities for merchandise and manpower, investment sources and opportunities, and resources for industrial use and consumption.

At present, less than one-third of South Korea's total international economic activity—a substantial portion but a far cry from what it used to be fifteen years ago—is done with the United States. South Korea even seeks opportunities of economic exchange with the communist powers in Asia including the Soviet Union and the People's Republic of China. South Korea's economic expansion, coupled with the diversification of international economic activities, is bound to contribute to freeing South Korea from heavy economic dependence upon the United States.

A third change can be seen in the growth of self-confidence and assertiveness among the South Korean people in general and its officials in particular. Obviously, one major source of this confidence is its rapidly expanding economy. At the same time, they do recognize that South Korea will ultimately have to bear the primary burden of defending itself against the North Korean military threat and securing the capability to deter an armed invasion. The anxiety felt by the South Korean officials during the early years of the Carter administration gave rise to the realization that U.S.-South Korean relations are too heavily dependent upon a particular U.S. administration that happens to be in power at a given time and that South Korea should be prepared for the contingency that U.S. security assistance might not be as readily forthcoming as it has been.

However, to say that there has been a change in the nature of the Korea-American alliance is not to mean either that the continued validity of the alliance is being questioned or that the relationship between the two countries will develop into one of near symmetry. South Korea will continue to require American arms, air and naval support, and intelligence and strategic assistance. A substantial portion of Korea's trade will continue to be carried out with the United States.

For the United States, Korea will remain as a strategically important area in its overall military posture in Asia and the Pacific. It is also emerging as a major market for its commercial goods and arms exports. It is difficult to anticipate this relationship undergoing a radical and fundamental change in the near future. Whatever change that has taken place, and that is likely to take place, would be adjustments—albeit significant ones—made to be more suitable to the changed world situation as well as to the domestic conditions of each of the partners within the basic alliance framework of the earlier years.

Chapter 3

The Emerging Triangle III: The North Korean Nuclear Issue

North Korean Policy Toward
the United States and Nuclear Weapons

Nineteen Months: The North Korean Nuclear Crisis of 1993–94

Fast Forward, 2020

North Korea, Today

The Korea Focus: The Influence of the Major Powers

A New Triangle Takes Shape:
Korean Attitudes Toward the U.S. and the PRC

The Unification Question

Conclusion

Chapter 3

The Emerging Triangle III: The North Korean Nuclear Issue[74]

North Korean Policy Toward the United States and Nuclear Weapons

Today is the third and final segment of our "mini-series" on the emerging triangular relationship among the United States, China, and Korea. In the first episode, we examined Korea-China ties, those that date back the farthest, thus making China the veritable "Big Man on the Peninsula." Then yesterday we looked at the growing importance of the Korea-U.S. relationship, from its rather unlikely origin of shipwrecks and plundering to the more harmonious present. Today I will attempt to "close the loop," or in this case triangle, on our survey of U.S.-China-Korea ties and where we may expect things to go from here. I will start with a look at recent changes in the North Korea-United States relations.

One of the most remarkable developments in the post-Cold War period has been the evolution of North Korean policy toward the United States. Until the end of the 1980s, the U. S. was depicted as the arch-enemy not only of North Korea but also of all of the socialist world. Expressions like "U.S. imperialist aggressors," "war mongering wolves," and "Western

---

74. Edwin O. Reischauer Memorial Lectures, April 3, 1998.

big-nose" are just a few of the unflattering epithets Pyongyang routinely reserved for Uncle Sam.

In North Korea's view, the United States was what kept it from victory, and thus reunification, in the Korean War. Since then, the U.S. helped South Korea to survive and thrive. The United States loomed particularly threatening not only with its generous military assistance to the South but also with the deployment of its troops and weapons, including tactical nuclear weapons.

With the end of the Cold War, however, Pyongyang recognized both the need and opportunity to improve its relationship with Washington. This became especially important after South Korea normalized its relations with the Soviet Union and China. North Korea could not let these new ties go unanswered. Furthermore, Pyongyang began to see the usefulness of a continued U.S. troop presence in Korea. In its absence, South Korea, with the economic capability to expand its own military power and a more aggressive attitude toward the North, could potentially be even more threatening.

Washington, for its part, was feeling left out of the normalization process. China and the Soviet Union each had relationships with both Koreas, and even Japan seemed about ready to jump on the "cross-recognition" bandwagon. Meanwhile, the U.S. was holding hands only with South Korea. Consequently, the prevailing sentiment of the two erstwhile enemies was that it was time for a change in their relationship. The meeting in January 1992 between Kim Yong Sun, North Korean Workers Party secretary of international affairs, and Arnold Kanter, U.S. undersecretary of state for political affairs, reflected this new possibility.

But the price of improving relations with the United States was high. The Bush administration wanted no less than for North Korea to give up the nuclear option, stop its missile development and sales, join the anti-terrorism conventions, and resume inter-Korea dialogue.

In an effort to address the U.S. requirements, North Korea took the step of signing the safeguards agreement with the IAEA and then ratifying it in the spring of 1992. The series of "ad hoc inspections" that followed that summer would prove to be its undoing, though; a "discrepancy" between the activities and materials North Korea had declared and those that were suspected by the IAEA inspectors was uncovered. So this gesture of goodwill toward the United States wound up backfiring, as it served only to magnify international suspicions about Pyongyang's nuclear program.

Next, in an unprecedented move, on March 12, 1993, the North Korean government declared that "in the supreme interest of the state," it was withdrawing from the Nuclear Non-Proliferation Treaty (NPT). This action represented a major gamble by North Korea as well as a serious foreign policy challenge to the United States. For one thing, the Clinton administration had been in office for less than seven weeks. But for the next 19 months, the two Koreas and the United States would become engulfed in a crisis that at one point almost ignited a military conflict.

Nineteen Months: The North Korean Nuclear Crisis of 1993–94

How did the situation unfold? The events known as the North Korean nuclear crisis of 1993–94 have been analyzed and written about from many perspectives. As one who was centrally involved in the making and implementation of the strategy to deal with it, I have my own biases and points of view. As I mentioned, the crisis persisted for 19 months. And, while I hardly think my account would make a best-seller or a blockbuster movie like say "48 Hours" or even "9 1/2 Weeks," these "19 months" did entail some amount of drama and intrigue, as I'll attempt to illustrate.

When we got the news of Pyongyang's announcement on withdrawing from the NPT, the President and his senior staff were attending a commencement ceremony at the Naval Academy in Chinhae, a naval port in southern Korea, and I was the only person left minding the store in Seoul. But I knew we had to come up with a strategy for dealing with the situation quickly, as the Kim Young-sam government was barely two weeks old and a system for handling a crisis like this one was yet to be put into place. The situation in Washington, D.C. was not much better. As the Clinton administration had been in office less than two months, many key positions in the government including the assistant secretaries dealing with Asia in the State and Defense departments had yet to be filled.

The details of the strategy, or "roadmap," as it was later called, were to be filled in during the ensuing weeks and months. But in brief outline, this is what went through my mind. Immediately, I wondered why the North Koreans opted to precipitate the crisis and why this particular timing. North Korea had been engaged in a nuclear weapons program for nearly two decades, and clearly, it was under enormous international pressure to accept the "special inspection" of the IAEA.

Furthermore, the nuclear issue proved to be a decisive obstacle to Pyongyang's effort to improve relations with both the United States and Japan. Now, instead of responding positively to North Korean overtures, the United States not only persuaded Japan to put off its negotiations with Pyongyang on diplomatic normalization but also decided to resume the "Team Spirit" military exercise, which Pyongyang found particularly objectionable and threatening.

In the meantime, the new government of President Kim Young-sam was making overtures of its own for the improvement of inter-Korean relations. One of the administration's first conciliatory gestures was the return to North Korea of Lee In-Mo, who had been incarcerated since the end of the Korean War for refusing to renounce his loyalty to the Pyongyang regime. Since Lee's return took place only one day before the announcement of the NPT withdrawal, it seemed clear that the decision on NPT had been made in advance and without reference to the South's overture.

There were two possible explanations for the North's provocative action. First, Pyongyang could have precipitated the crisis in order to avoid the IAEA special inspections and continue with its nuclear program. North Korea had been under enormous international pressure to fully open up its nuclear activities for inspection ever since the Bush Administration withdrew U.S. tactical nuclear weapons from Korea and persuaded South Korea to publicly renounce reprocessing and enrichment facilities. Furthermore, Pyongyang had signed a bilateral denuclearization declaration with South Korea in which it even promised: "reciprocal inspections" of each other's nuclear facilities. Why this sudden change of heart? To borrow another movie metaphor, Pyongyang may have decided that when the time for nuclear inspections finally came, it was not willing to go "the full monty" after all.

The other possible explanation was that Pyongyang might simply have wanted to make the most of what was a very difficult situation by using its nuclear leverage as a bargaining chip. In return for giving up the nuclear option, North Korea could expect to be compensated with nuclear reactors, alternative energy, and, above all, the privilege of negotiating directly with the United States and maybe establish relations with it. The answer to the question of which of the two explanations truly reflected Pyongyang's motives is unclear even today. It was even more difficult to answer at the beginning of the crisis.

I had three major concerns at the time. The first was the possibility of North Korea actually developing nuclear weapons, thereby changing the strategic equation in the Korean Peninsula. The second was the possibility that the international community (i.e., the United States) would react so strongly that war would break out in Korea. The third was the possibility that the North Korean nuclear program would touch off a race to develop nuclear weapons in South Korea and Japan.

The United States had similar concerns, although the priorities might have been somewhat different. It was concerned that, if not responded to effectively and resolutely, the North Korean decision unilaterally to withdraw from the NPT would be a serious blow to the global nonproliferation regime. It was also concerned that, if the North Korean nuclear program proceeded unchecked, it would have a very undesirable effect on the nuclear policy of South Korea and Japan. Furthermore, a North Korea armed with nuclear weapons and missiles would be a serious threat to the peace on the Korean Peninsula and particularly the 35,000 U.S. troops stationed there to keep that peace.

The first order of business, it was deemed, was to devise a strategy that would prevent an armed conflict on the Korean Peninsula while still effectively addressing the North Korean challenge. At the end of March, I traveled to Washington to discuss the problem. I found that leading members of the U.S. government were very receptive to my concerns and to my broad outline of how to respond. We agreed on what was to be known as a "carrot and stick" approach whereby we would try the dialogue route first and, if that proved futile, follow with the "stick." The rationale behind this approach was that it was important to make every effort to avoid an armed conflict before risking a war.

Another important reason for taking this approach rather than a more hardline stance was China. Since China as a permanent member of the United Nations Security Council had veto power, it was necessary to have Chinese cooperation (either an affirmative vote or at least an abstention) for the passage of any resolution on the issue. Securing this cooperation required convincing China that all peaceful means to resolve the issue had been exhausted. Therefore, from the point of view of the United States and South Korea, unless the military option was pursued from the beginning, taking the dialogue route first was both preferable and necessary.

In fact, China shared many of the same interests of the United States and South Korea, among them a nuclear-free Korean peninsula and concerns about the effect of North Korea's nuclear ambitions on Japan's nuclear policy. However, China also wanted to maintain what influence it had on North Korea. For this reason, China must have concluded that it could not be seen as taking a clear position against the North.

Instead, China took a neutral position, both in the IAEA and in the United Nations. In the IAEA, Beijing initially showed reluctance to have the North Korean issue referred to the UN Security Council, although ultimately, it acquiesced. Even after the issue was taken up by the Security Council, China kept urging both sides to resolve the issue through dialogue. It was particularly emphatic in wanting the United States to seek a negotiated settlement with North Korea.

There were probably two reasons for the position that China took at the time. First, Beijing could understand the North Korean sense of desperation and despair when China normalized its diplomatic ties with South Korea, but then there was no reciprocation in Pyongyang-Washington relations. Second, China was probably convinced from the outset of the crisis that what Pyongyang ultimately wanted was bargaining power rather than confrontation.

Throughout the 19-month period of the crisis, I think China played an important and constructive role. On April 22, 1993, I met Chinese Foreign Minister Qian Qichen in Bangkok on the occasion of an ESCAP conference and suggested that U.S.-North Korean talks could take place if China, in return, would agree not to veto a UN Security Council resolution calling on the North to comply with international nuclear inspections and stay in the NPT system. This suggestion was made, of course, after close consultation with the United States. Subsequently, China did not veto the resolution, which enabled the Security Council and the United States to take up the issue.

At each turn of events during the crisis, China exercised its influence over North Korea sparingly and in a way that it thought was feasible and consistent with its wish to maintain that influence. The most critical test of Chinese policy came in early June of 1994. At the time, the situation was tense and war clouds were gathering as North Korea adamantly refused to allow IAEA inspectors in after withdrawing 8,000 rods of spent nuclear fuel earlier that year.

The United States and South Korea had all but given up hope of resolving the issue by negotiation and sought a sanctions resolution of the Security Council. Their determination to take stern action was so strong that if a Security Council resolution proved to be unobtainable, they were prepared to impose sanctions outside of the UN framework (probably by the United States, South Korea, and Japan). In the meantime, Pyongyang was threatening, in its characteristic way of brinkmanship, that a sanctions resolution by the UN Security Council would be considered an act of war. And the United States, for its part, was preparing for the possibility of a large-scale war in Korea.

In a last-ditch effort to resolve the problem without military confrontation, I traveled back to Beijing on June 9 to solicit Chinese cooperation. I told my Chinese counterparts that we (South Korea and the United States) had sought a negotiated settlement and had exhausted all means of achieving it. I emphasized that the only way to avoid a vote on a sanctions resolution in the Security Council, and thus avert a military conflict on the Korean Peninsula, would be for China to tell the North Koreans that they could not count on a Chinese veto. Subsequently, it was learned that the Beijing government indeed told the North Koreans that China may not be able to veto the resolution against strong international opinion and that they had better take action to defuse the situation.

The events that followed showed that the Chinese message, unpleasant as it must have been to Pyongyang, had the desired impact. Within a matter of a few days, former U.S. President Jimmy Carter was invited to North Korea. In a meeting with President Kim Il Sung on June 16, Carter obtained the North Korean leader's promise that the IAEA inspectors would be allowed back into the country and the high level U.S.-North Korean negotiations would be resumed. Kim Il Sung also accepted South Korean President Kim Young-sam's proposal, conveyed to him by President Carter, for an inter-Korea summit meeting. So in sum, without the timely intervention of China, it is questionable whether a military confrontation would have been averted at that time.

The Geneva "Agreed Framework": Ultimately, the United States concluded an "Agreed Framework" with North Korea. It was signed in Geneva on October 21, 1994, after on-again/off-again negotiations interrupted by war scares stretching over seventeen months. The agreement had both merits and demerits.

Critics were quick to note that the agreement allowed at least several years to pass before the IAEA could conduct the "special inspection" of the undeclared nuclear waste site. What's more, the agreement "rewarded" North Korea with benefits such as energy supply and light water reactors for its defiance of the IAEA. But considering that it was the special inspection issue that prompted the controversy between Pyongyang and the IAEA, it was not surprising that the Agreed Framework was faulted for failing to deal satisfactorily with the IAEA complaints at even high financial cost to the international community.

On the positive side, the agreement put an end to the crisis situation, which could have brought about a destructive military clash. It also succeeded in freezing the North Korean nuclear program and activities, in effect removing the possibility of its engaging in a nuclear weapons development program. Finally, it gave North Korea a stake in implementing the agreement. The prospect of receiving heavy oil and securing light water reactors gave Pyongyang an incentive to "behave," at least a little better than before. This probably explains why the North Koreans uncharacteristically apologized for the 1996 incursion of a submarine vessel into South Korean waters. The potential of losing the benefits also helped to restrain North Korean reaction in the defection case of Hwang Jang-yop.

In the meantime, North Korea has kept its nuclear program frozen, has allowed the IAEA continued inspection of its nuclear facilities and has had the withdrawn fuel rods encased for safe-keeping. The agreement also induced Pyongyang to participate in the four-party talks, which began in December 1997 after much hesitation. Pyongyang is yet to implement the inter-Korea dialogue provision of the agreement. But there is no question that the relatively restrained behavior of North Korea since 1994 can be attributed to the Geneva agreement with the United States.

During much of the negotiation, the United States was apprehensive that the South Korean government's position showed inconsistency, moving back and forth between hard and soft lines. In fact, Seoul was initially concerned with the possibility of the United States taking a rash (military) action against North Korea. But in the end, Seoul's complaint was that the United States was too soft in dealing with the North. So although the ROK government ultimately accepted the agreed framework, it did so only after fierce internal debate and with much reluctance.

Fast Forward, 2020

With the 1994 Geneva Agreed Framework, North Korean nuclear program and activity were frozen and the IAEA monitoring was resumed fast forward, 2010, twenty-six years later. We now know that the Geneva Agreed Framework did not resolve the North Korean nuclear issue. North Korea cheated. Defying international (UN) sanctions, they restarted their nuclear weapons-making, have produced dozens of nuclear bombs and now possess them together with long and short-range missiles for their delivery. North Korea proclaims it is a nuclear weapons state and threatens with them not only South Korea but also other countries, including the United States, Japan, and China. It demands to have nuclear talks with the United States as a nuclear weapons state.

In South Korea today (2020), there are two opposing views on North Korean nuclear weapons. The Moon government and the government party emphasize North Korea actually seeks nuclear weapons for defensive and deterrence purposes. They believe North Korea is arming itself with nuclear weapons because it feels insecure. They say that Kim Jong Un has made a strategic choice to give up nuclear weapons and focus on economic development in return for accommodating gestures such as relaxing or lifting sanctions and removing nuclear threats against it.

They also say that the international pressure (i.e., economic sanctions) worked and North Korea will ultimately accept denuclearization. They argue that peace and reconciliation are most important and, therefore, the United States and its allies, including South Korea, should adopt a soft approach toward North Korea.

On the other hand, many experts, former government officials, conservatives, and most opposition parties argue that the Moon government is either deceived by Kim Jong Un or colluding with it to mislead the South Korean people. They worry that U.S. President Trump might make a deal (e.g., North Korea giving up ICBMs for retaining nuclear weapons) which would enable North Korea to make a *fait accompli* of its being a nuclear weapons state.

Kim Jong Un's objectives in developing nuclear weapons are: To become a nuclear weapons state, to weaken U.S.-ROK alliance, to make American troops withdraw, ultimately take over South Korea ("after reunification"), and to dismantle sanctions regime (starting with South Korea, China, and Russia).

Some people compare the current situation ("nuclear crisis" or "peace momentum") to the first nuclear crisis (1993–94), Comparing the North Korean nuclear crisis in 1993–94 and the situation now, we can make the following observations:

1. In 1993 to 1994, North Korea's nuclear program was still a fledgling one, but now it probably possesses dozens of nuclear weapons, being manufactured with both the plutonium and highly enriched uranium (HEU) programs. North Korean nuclear capability has grown exponentially. North Korea is believed to have dozens (50 to 60) of nuclear weapons. The South Korean government of Moon Jae-in is much more accommodating

to North Korea, while the Trump government in the United States places greater emphasis on political calculations than strategic considerations.

2. In 1993 and 94, China, even as it was reluctant in putting explicit pressure on North Korea, it nevertheless played constructive role in trying to resolve the crisis, China is more involved in the North Korean nuclear issue now but, at the same time, more protective of North Korea and therefore permissive regarding North Korean nuclear weapons.

3. In the 1990s, North Korea was afraid of the UN Security Council's sanctions resolution, but now, after several such sanctions, North Korea seems unafraid of them and has become quite defiant.

4. In 1993 to 94, the United States was willing to and did play a leading role in dealing with the issue and negotiating with North Korea. During the Obama years, it was reluctant to play that role in the name of "strategic patience" and instead tried to leave the initiative and main burden to other countries, mainly China and South Korea. That attitude was changing somewhat, although too late in the second Obama Administration.

5. In 1993 and 94, North Korea denied and tried to conceal its nuclear program. Now it boasts of and even exaggerates such a program, and tries to use it as bargaining leverage.

So why is North Korea boasting, even exaggerating, and openly threatening with nuclear weapons and missiles with possible attack on the United States, South Korea, and other countries in between? Why is it not trying, as other late nuclear weapons developers had done, to hide, deny, or at least not flaunting their weapons, instead of boasting, exaggerating, threatening their use against their "enemies?" As far as we can tell, Kim Jong Un is trying to make North Korea's possession of nuclear weapons a *fait accompli* and to make the red line or goal post of North Korean denuclearization further away.

In addition, Kim would also want to uplift its bargaining position by raising the price of bargaining; to propagandize its (his) accomplishments; to wage psychological warfare vis-à-vis South Korea by implanting a sense of insecurity and fear, and to sew doubts on U.S. deterrence capability and resolve among its allies.

During the past three decades, both China and the United States paid insufficient attention to the seriousness of the North Korean nuclear problem. China has been more concerned about keeping the North Korean regime afloat than stopping North Korea's nuclear program. The United States has been too preoccupied with and diverted to the Middle East and the Iranian nuclear issue. Only now, they seem to be giving the amount of weight and attention to the North Korean problem that it deserves and demands. China, in particular, has joined the United States, Japan, and South Korea in supporting a strong sanctions resolution (to wit, Res. 2270) at the UN Security Council and vows to implement it fully and thoroughly. Even though China will not go so far or do anything to undo the North Korean regime, and even though there are plenty of skeptical views on how far and how long Beijing would go with its vows of implementing the sanctions faithfully, it is nevertheless true that China in fact has been cooperating in inflicting more pains to North Korea with the sanctions than any time before.

What are the reasons for this important change of stance, at least partially, on the part of Beijing regarding North Korean nuclear weapons? There are probably four reasons: 1) China is indeed beginning to recognize and feel the threat of North Korean nuclear weapons, both directly and by way of prompting the United States and its allies to mobilize and strengthen their military response; 2) Beijing is furious with North Korea for slapping China's hand by conducting nuclear and missile tests despite its ardent persuasion, and wishes to send a strong signal and "teach a lesson" as China is wont to do with other countries; 3) Contrary to the earlier thinking that joining a strong sanctions move in the UN Security Council would compromise whatever influence China has over North Korea, in fact strong sanctions would strengthen China's hand vis-à-vis North Korea as it still has the leverage of either strongly strangling North Korea's neck or relaxing it somewhat. Finally, by cooperating on this issue with the United States, Beijing would feel that it has a better chance of dissuading the U.S. from pursuing policies that it considers disadvantageous to it, such as on missile defense.

North Korea, Today

Over the years, North Korea has shown three tactical patterns: brinkmanship, salami tactic, and back-loading key concessions. After several years of bragging and blustering, Kim Jong Un is employing a double track tactic: provocations with missile tests and peace offensive. It is trying to take advantage and make use of the friendly Moon government in the South.

The Moon government seems to be in the position of "coaching" Kim Jong Un on how to deal with U.S. President Trump. Together with North Korea, President Moon promotes the so-called "End of War in the Korean Peninsula" Declaration, a move that is supported by China and Russia. They obviously expect that such a declaration will weaken the rationale for continued maintenance of U.S. troops in South Korea and even the U.S.-ROK alliance itself.

Trump, on his part, is mainly interested in self-promotion and gain political benefits by appearing to "resolve" the North Korean nuclear issue. While he has rather low regards for allies and alliances, he places emphasis on his political needs and exhibits impulsiveness as he deals with Kim Jong Un and the nuclear issue. Trump wants to claim he has brought peace on the Korean Peninsula. He raised the tension, then takes credit for lowering the tension. The cost of this gambit is depriving what Koreans call "security consciousness" by fostering false complacency.

As the Presidential election in the United States approaches, Kim Jong Un is now in a position to do a political favor by making a deal on nuclear weapons and missiles with President Trump, a deal that Trump can spin and tout as a great political achievement. Even if it is a half-baked deal (legitimizing the nuclear status quo of North Korea), the Moon government will most probably welcome it as a peace bringing measure.

As of now and for the time being, neither Kim nor Trump will want to go back to the trigger happy appearances, war-mongering attitudes or blustering ways as shown in 2017. It would not be in the political interest of either one. Whether they like it or not, they seem to be in the same boat. Trump may want to get out of the jam by making a deal, such as exchanging the ICBM for a nuclear status quo. They can both claim it as a great, tremendous achievement and success.

The Korea Focus: The Influence of the Major Powers

It will be useful at this point to review the basic goals and policies of the major powers—the U.S., China, Japan, and Russia—in relation to the Korean Peninsula. The United States: Starting with the United States, its goals can be summarized in about 7 main points, as follows:

1. Maintain peace and stability on the Korean Peninsula
2. Prevent weapons of mass destruction (WMDs), including missiles
3. Secure and maintain a handle and influence on Korean affairs
4. Maintain U.S. troops and keep Korea as a forward base
5. Contain and/or balance Russia and China as the case may be
6. Protect, reassure and balance Japan
7. Keep South Korea as a showcase of democracy and economic development

In order to achieve these goals, the United States has adopted the following basic policies:

1. A one and one-half Korea policy whereby the United States would maintain the "special relationship" with South Korea, including a military alliance while establishing a working relationship with North Korea
2. A "soft landing" policy which is neither clearly explained nor understood
3. Improvement of relations with North Korea while providing food aid. In this connection, there is a continuing debate on the question of lifting economic sanctions
4. Strengthening the alliance with Japan; cooperation with China;

and a sort of benign neglect of Russia
5. Emphasis on KEDO, and separate negotiations on other WMDs, including missiles
6. Emphasis on four-party talks

China: China, for its part, shares many of the same objectives as the United States regarding the Korean peninsula. A summary of China's goals might include:

Goals:

1. Peace and stability on the Korean Peninsula—keeping the balance between North and South; avoiding any conflicts which China could be drawn into
2. Preventing the collapse of North Korea—a greater interest in keeping North Korea afloat than other powers; providing necessary aid to this end
3. Preventing the dominance of Korea by another power (U.S.)
4. Preventing a stream of North Korean refugees across its border
5. Non-nuclear Korean Peninsula
6. Concern over nationalism of ethnic Koreans
7. Continued economic benefits
8. Prevent anti-China containment

Policies:

1. Cooperate with the United States and South Korea as much as feasible and necessary, especially on the nuclear issue and on peace structure on the Korean Peninsula
2. Encourage U.S.-North Korea relations
3. Express misgivings and show sensitivity on U.S.-Japan alliance (especially on the possibility of expanding Japan's regional role and possible rearmament by Japan)
4. Active involvement in four-party talks

5. Expression of ambivalent attitude toward U.S. troops in Korea
6. Wait and see the prospects and process of the Korean unification process

Japan has an equivocal attitude toward North Korea and the unification issue. Japan wants to improve relations with Pyongyang. It is an active participant in the KEDO process. But it has been at best passive in providing food aid to North Korea since 1995 when it gave substantial assistance. Now it does not want to be seen as towing the U.S. line and having to assume an excessive burden. Nor does it wish to move ahead of South Korea, which does not want to see Japan move too fast or too far. But it will be difficult to maintain this passive policy for too long. Sooner or later, Japan will find a rationale to provide aid and improve relations with North Korea. Japan will want to do this in consultation with the United States and South Korea but not necessarily in lockstep with them.

Japan's goals and policies may be summarized as follows:

Goals:

1. Peace and stability
2. Status quo attitude toward unification
3. Security: Korea as a buffer; U.S. troops in Japan; Korea as a potential threat
4. Non-nuclearization of Korea
5. Prevent Chinese dominance of Korea

Policies:

1. Participate in KEDO process
2. Seek negotiations with North Korea on the normalization of relations
3. On South Korea-Japan security relations—lukewarm although positive

4. Maintain a strong alliance with the United States and U.S. bases in Japan
5. Support of the United States (including rear-area support in case of war on the Korean Peninsula) on the Korea question

Russia: Russia's main concern regarding the Korean issue is not to be left out of the process. Hence, in 1994, it proposed an international conference in connection with the North Korean nuclear issue. Russia is not happy with the four-party proposal, which excludes both Russia and Japan. Until 1995, Russian relations with Pyongyang worsened to the extent that Russia decided not to renew its security treaty with North Korea. Since then, Moscow has been making an effort to mend fences. Nevertheless, Russia has limited resources with which to help North Korea. And North Korea, for its part, is concentrating its attention on the United States as a source of support and aid.

A summary of Russian goals and policies includes:

Goals (defined more in negative terms):

1. Not to be left out of the process
2. Economic
3. Maintain good relations with the U.S., Japan, China
4. Least interested in status quo
5. Prevent U.S. or Chinese dominance

Policies:

1. Mend fences with North Korea—1995–97
2. Unhappy with four-party talks; advocacy of multi-party international conference
3. Acquiesce to Sino-Russian rapprochement—although having misgivings on the rise of China

A New Triangle Takes Shape:
Korean Attitudes Toward the U.S. and the PRC

Having touched on the major powers' policies and goals regarding the two Koreas, I would like now to comment here on the changing attitudes of Koreans, North and South, toward the two major powers.

The first observation that comes to mind is that old adage: Familiarity breeds contempt. For North Korea, China has been a close ally for the past half-century, while the U.S. has been the enemy. Similarly, for South Korea, the United States has been closely aligned, while China was seen as an enemy. It is ironic, then, that today, China seems to rank more favorably in South Korea than in the North. It is possible, although difficult to verify, that China ranks even above the United States to some South Koreans. During the 1988 Olympics in Seoul, for example, some South Korean spectators cheered more enthusiastically for both the Russian and Chinese players than the American athletes.

Is the level of anti-American sentiment in South Korea rising? Negative attitudes toward the United States can be found particularly among people who belong to two opposite ends of the ideological spectrum. There are those on the left, who have been critical of the United States all along, and who blame the U.S. for the continued division of the country, meddling in domestic politics, failing to prevent the Kwangju massacre in 1980, and "dependency" of the Korean economy on the world (particularly the U.S.) economy as demonstrated in the recent foreign currency crisis. This group is also resentful of what they consider to be an inequality between the two countries, as exemplified in the Status of Forces Agreement (SOFA).

On the other hand, those on the right, who until recent years have been generally "pro-American" in their attitude, are concerned that the United States is too soft in dealing with North Korea. They fear the U.S. may seek accommodation with the North, bypassing South Korea and perhaps against its best interest. This feeling among some Koreans that the United States is not tough enough to our communist foes is nothing new. Syngman Rhee frequently complained that the United States was too soft on communism and communist countries. This group also feels that the United States, unlike in the past, pursues only its self-interest (especially in the economic arena), ignoring or sacrificing the interest of South Korea, its close ally and friend.

In spite of these rather entrenched attitudes on the part of some, I would not go so far as to say that anti-American sentiment in South Korea is either pervasive or rising. One hears anti-American slogans on university campuses much less frequently than before. And the South Korean people (including the media) are beginning to realize that nations do indeed act in their own self-interest most of the time and that sometimes this is compatible with another country's interest, and sometimes it is not.

As for China, South Koreans consider the Chinese domination of centuries past a distant memory. They find the new relationship that was recently established with China gratifying and generally satisfactory. Not having experienced Chinese domination in the way North Korea has in recent decades, there is no reason for them to be resentful of an "overbearing" China.

One may find a symmetrical attitude among North Koreans vis-à-vis the United States. Although it is impossible to distinguish between the attitudes of government officials and the general public in North Korea, it is possible to conclude that, despite the anti-American propaganda of the past, North Koreans generally have a favorable attitude toward the United States. This is in fact borne out by the attitudes exhibited by those North Koreans who have had contact with the outside world. Given that the U.S. is considered the only ticket out of the current economic troubles, it is reasonable to assume that North Koreans have all but forgotten that the United States was the war-mongering imperialist power that they learned to hate.

By contrast, China must be looked upon in North Korea with mixed feelings. Although it was the savior of the North Korean regime at the time of the Korean War and continues to be its last back-stop, Beijing has had its share of troubles with the North. Chinese troops were stationed in North Korea after the Korean War until 1958. Even after that, China continued to exercise influence in North Korea through pro-Chinese North Koreans, military assistance, and ideological guidance. Although Kim Il Sung tried to minimize Chinese involvement in North Korean affairs by manipulating the

Sino-Soviet conflict, some degree of Chinese influence was unavoidable.

North Korea was particularly disappointed with China when it reached a rapprochement with the United States in 1972. But even that disappointment paled in comparison to the anger and sense of betrayal that North Korea felt when, in 1992, China followed the Soviet Union in recognizing South Korea. Also, although settlement of territorial and boundary issues was reached in 1963, because of the geographical proximity of the two countries, there have always been border troubles, mostly minor but some major ones.

This is not to say that a strong or rising wind of anti-Chinese sentiment is detected among the North Koreans. The important point, however, is that the previous alignments—China and North Korea on one side and the United States and South Korea on the other—have little meaning today, at least in terms of the prevailing sentiments in the North and the South. This is another dimension of factors that makes the triangular relationship among Korea, China, and the United States more complex and fluid.

The Unification Question[75]

In trying to figure what will happen with North Korea in the post-Kim Il Sung era, there are numerous factors to consider. Will the power base of the new leadership be strong enough to maintain the stability of the regime? Will this leadership recognize that it is in its own interest to engage in the regional and global order? More immediately and urgently, will the leadership be able to cope with the serious economic difficulties and severe shortages in food and energy? What are the implications of all of these factors for North Korea's relationship with South Korea and the rest of the World?

There are two main tasks, which appear to be key to the North Korean leadership's success: first, tackling the country's economic problems; and second, breaking out of diplomatic isolation. These challenges pose a difficult dilemma for North Korea: Pyongyang must decide whether it will

---

75. This (unification) issue will be dealt with in greater detail in Section 5 of this book.

open up its society and risk contamination or remain closed and continue to fall behind.

To be sure, a policy of openness and reform is the only choice for relieving North Korea's economic problems. But unlike China and Vietnam, North Korea still exhibits a considerable degree of resistance to the introduction of a market economy. It remains to be seen whether the leadership in Pyongyang has the courage, wisdom, and ability to embark upon the needed reforms.

In order to escape its diplomatic isolation, North Korea has placed top policy priority on the improvement of its relations with the United States. Once progress has been made in U.S.-North Korea relations, Pyongyang is likely to move quickly towards Japan for diplomatic recognition and economic assistance. Increased contacts and exchanges with the outside world, particularly the U.S., could pose a potential threat to North Korea since such exposure will inevitably change the chemistry of North Korean society. One can only presume that North Korea will attempt a controlled opening to the extent that it will not undermine the stability of the regime itself. No one knows if this course of action will be possible.

North Korea still retains the military capability to threaten the peace and stability of the Korean Peninsula and beyond. What may come next? There are several possibilities. North Korea may continue to muddle through its economic difficulties with its basic political and economic system intact. A more development-minded, although equally authoritarian, the government may come in, by either a military coup or a palace coup. This new regime may agree to an accommodation with the South, leading to gradual reconciliation and even socio-economic cooperation. Alternatively, the landing may not be that "soft" after all. North Korea may experience either a sudden or gradual collapse with uncertain and possibly highly destabilizing consequences.

As for the major powers, there is widespread suspicion, in both Koreas, that they actually prefer the status quo of a divided state. Each may fear that a reunified Korea would fall under the dominance of one of the other major powers. Or they may fear that a reunified Korea could be a threat in itself. But the major concern is probably that the actual process of reunification could be highly destabilizing and possibly violent. That said, if the main current is toward reunification, either by the decisions of the Koreans themselves or by force of international events, it will be difficult or unlikely that any one or more of the big powers will go out of its way to prevent reunification from taking place. I will have a separate section (#5) on the unification issue, which will deal with the possible opportunities and obstacles to an early unification of Korea.

Conclusion

In sum, we started our discussion with the possibility that in a global chessboard of the major powers, the United States and China are in a competition if not conflict with each other for domination of Korea. While Korea is divided, divided domination can exist. Once Korea is unified, however, the question arises as to who or anyone will dominate, and indeed any outcome is possible.

Ordinarily, when we talk about the "Korean triangle," we think of Korea squeezed between China and Japan. Indeed, like Poland which suffered between Germany and Russia, Korea through the centuries had to deal with the contending ambitions and influences of China and Japan. For that reason, a Korea-Japan-China triangle portends dangers for Korea. It will be difficult for Korea to stay aloof in the Sino-Japanese competition. Neither will it be desirable for Korea to align with either of the two neighboring powers exclusively.

In the absence of a multilateral structure for regional peace and cooperation such as those found in Europe, therefore, the Korea-China-U.S. triangle presents both a danger and opportunity for Korea. It can hope to stay clear of potential rivalry and conflict between China and Japan. It is an opportunity because a close involvement of the United States in this region will give Korea room to maneuver among and between the powers.

It is fortuitous that a careful look at the policies and aspirations, past and present, of the two major powers—China and the United States—suggests that the picture is much more complex than a simple chess game of a zero-sum nature.

Even as both powers prefer the stability of the status quo on the

Korean Peninsula, they have to be prepared for a major change. The new situation will require both competition and cooperation. At the same time, this expected Sino-American competition will provide a challenge to Korea, divided or unified. Surely it will require close consultation and coordination, especially between Korea and the United States, whether Korea is two or one.

For the moment, common interests between China and the United States seem to outweigh conflicting interests. And it is by no means inevitable that China and the United States must find themselves on a collision course over Korea even in the future.

Whether they do would depend on developments within the Korean Peninsula, relationships among the major powers, and the nature of international relations, which may or may not repeat the power politics of the past. New elements in the equation could be the ability of the Koreans to run their own affairs, including unification and governance, the capacity of international and regional regimes to regulate relations among nations, and the evolution of the Chinese society and U.S. policy.

There is no question that as North and South Korea are coming to evolve into one entity in Chinese and American thinking, the three powers will form a triangle. It is to be seen whether these three elements—Korea, China, and the United States—portend more hostility than amicability and greater flexibility than rigidity in their relationships with one another.

An Uneasy Triangle:
Korea Between China and Japan

The Geopolitical Situation in Northeast Asia

Korea's Role in China-Japan-Korea Triangle

The Northeast Asia Triangle and North Korean Nuclear Issue

Rise of China and Resurgent Nationalism in Northeast Asia

Chapter 4

An Uneasy Triangle: Korea Between China and Japan

When I was asked to give a talk here at IHJ (International House of Japan) on the occasion of its 60th founding anniversary under the broad umbrella subject of Japan's role in the world, it seemed that the three countries—China, Japan, and Korea—were on the verge of negotiating and even in due course coming to an agreement on a three-nation FTA (free trade agreement). The leaders of the three countries agreed at their summit meeting held in Beijing in May, 2012, to discuss and negotiate a trilateral FTA. Since then, however, the relations among the three countries have grown quite uneasy and turbulent, with the explosion of nationalistic sentiments and aggravation of territorial disputes.

Today, I wish to talk about the triangular relationships in Northeast Asia, with a particular focus on Korea's tightrope-walking relations and roles between the two big powers, namely China and Japan. In the second decade of the 21st century, the three major Northeast Asian countries—China, Japan, and (South) Korea—which share geographic proximity and cultural tradition, are moving in two opposite directions; cooperation and integration on one hand, and conflict and disintegration on the other. The move toward integration is aided by increasing economic interdependence, the accompanying imperative to cooperate, and expansion of social networks and people exchanges among the three countries. The move toward disintegration is abetted by even stronger elements of nationalistic sentiment, historical baggage as well as diplomatic responses and counter-responses, and contending territorial claims. The changing power configuration among the three countries—as China is in the process of surpassing Japan in national power and international standing—and Korea is trying to move from a position of distant third to one that is as much close to a coequal to the other two as possible—serves both as a factor that requires greater cooperation among the three countries and, at the same time, as one that fosters greater suspicion and perceived need to counter and check the others. China's support for and shielding of North Korea, which threatens the rest of the region with nuclear weapons, long-range missiles, provocative behavior, and socioeconomic insolvency, is a cause for Japan's and South Korea's concern and frustration. China used to consider Japan's and South Korea's alliances with the United States as a necessary evil to maintain regional stability and to prevent Japan's rearmament. China, however, now regards the U.S. alliance system as mainly aiming at containing and encircling it, not at contributing to enhancing regional integration in Northeast Asia. China disparages it as a legacy of the Cold War. As such, in the absence of a viable security structure and architecture in this sub-region, the alliances and alignments have strained as much as they have stabilized the relationships among the Northeast Asian countries.

The Geopolitical Situation in Northeast Asia

At the moment, the geopolitical situation in Northeast Asia is complicated in particular by the persistent tension arising from galvanized nationalism and territorial disputes between and among China, Japan, and Korea. Japan seems nervous about the implications of China's rapidly developing economy and potential military might. In the post-World War II period, Japan, which had been defeated in the war, was defensive and expressed remorse about its past colonial and militaristic behavior. However, Japan today is run by the leaders of a younger generation who refuse to feel responsible or apologetic about colonial and militaristic past.

China, which had gone through decades of civil war, ideological upheavals, economic hardships, and international isolation, has now become the world's second-largest economy and looks toward being a member of the so-called G-2 with the United States. China now worries about Japan's growing military capabilities and trends of resurging nationalism. The persistence of 19th and 20th centuries' geopolitics in Asia is especially inimical to the creation and development of a regional community on either a regional (East Asian) or sub-regional (Northeast Asian) basis as what has been witnessed in Europe. In an environment replete with geopolitical rivalries, nations tend to opt for unilateralism or bilateralism rather than multilateralism. By the same token, they incline toward nationalism at the expense of regionalism, internationalism, or globalism. Rifts among Northeast Asian countries portend a danger not only of torpedoing the East Asian community-building process but also, at a minimum, of leaving the leadership and initiatives almost entirely to their Southeast Asian neighbors.

Korea's Role in China-Japan-Korea Triangle

Today, I would like to focus on what role Korea can and does play in the China-Japan-Korea triangle and then speculate on the prospects for evolution of their triangular relationships in the future. During the past two millennia, Korea, a peninsula located at the northeastern corner of China and across a strait from Japan, has maintained a separate national entity linguistically, culturally, emotionally, and politically. In the process, it faced encroachments, invasions, even occupation, and otherwise dominating influence from its powerful neighbors, namely China and Japan. In many ways, Korea's fate was comparable to that of Poland in Europe, sandwiched and squeezed by the powerful neighbors of Russia and Germany.

For many centuries, Korea had been invaded and occupied by successive Chinese dynasties. In the late 16th century, Japan waged a full-scale and devastating invasion of the Korean Peninsula. In the 20th century, Korea was subjected to Japanese domination and colonialism, followed by the division of the country into the North and the South, which were occupied by the Soviet and American troops respectively. As soon as the two Koreas became independent, they turned to fighting a fratricidal proxy war, supported respectively by the United States for the South, and the Soviet Union and China for the North. As a result of this tragic historical legacy, both young and old Koreans in the still divided parts of their fatherland, have come to harbor a strong sense of being aggrieved and wronged, and thus a fierce sense of nationalism. While nationalism in China and Japan has both defensive and offensive tendencies, Korean nationalism primarily tends to be defensive and retributive in character.

Even though Korea as a country remains divided, the South has become an economic powerhouse and diplomatic stronghold as a leading member of the G-20. (This is also despite the fact that it is threatened by the North's nuclear and missile programs.) It has also become an actively leading partner in managing international organizations such as the United Nations. As South Korea has moved up in national power and regional status from a distant third, among the three Northeast Asian countries of China, Japan, and Korea, to a bona fide member of the trio that cannot be simply overlooked or passed over, there emerge various tactical and strategic questions of how to deal with its two powerful neighbors—China and Japan.

Let me now talk about the relations between the three nations in connection with specific issue areas. First, the issue of North Korea's nuclear weapons program. The issue of how to deal with North Korea is a persistent thorn in relations between China, Japan, and (South) Korea. Since the time is limited today, and this is such a complex issue, I will not describe in detail the position of each country but merely touch on the problem briefly. It is clear, that all the three countries would like to see North Korea denuclearized and prevent it from becoming a bona fide nuclear weapons state, but they have respectively different objectives and approaches in handling the issue.

The problem also lies with the fact that sometimes a country's goals tend to contradict one another. For example, China wants to achieve a denuclearized North Korea but it also wants to keep the North Korean regime alive and to manage the situation on the Korean peninsula to prevent military clashes. Japan and Korea tend to side with each other but for the Japanese, the issue of Japanese abductees prevents them from making progress on the issue. For South Koreans they cannot imagine any scenario of resolving the North Korean issue that does not involve them—for fear of being left out of important decisions made by neighboring countries—this is a product of Korea's tragic history.

The Northeast Asia Triangle and North Korean Nuclear Issue

Over the past two decades, North Korea's nuclear weapons program has been an issue of major concern for its surrounding countries including South Korea, Japan, and China. Despite the Geneva Agreed Framework of 1994 which placed a lid on its nuclear program, North Korea restarted it several years later and has now become a de facto nuclear weapons state having conducted tests twice each in 2006 and 2009. Since 2003, five countries including China, the United States, Russia, Japan, and South Korea have tried to persuade the North through the six-party talks to abandon its nuclear program, but without much success or outcome.

China has taken the position that the North Korean nuclear problem should be resolved through dialogue by peaceful means. China believes that, even if it might take a long time, the parties concerned, especially the United States and South Korea, should not rush into excessive pressure or coercive measures. Why does China insist on a soft approach toward North Korea? In order to encourage North Korea to give up its nuclear weapons, China has to increase the level of pressure. But too strong pressure could in turn lead to the demise of the Northern regime. Thus, if China wants to sustain the Pyongyang regime, it has no choice but to respond softly to the nuclear problem and react also gently to other issues involving North Korea.

China sometimes appears to step up pressure on the North Korean nuclear issue, but only when it is encountered with an urge from the United States. For example, the *New York Times* reported last month that in November 2010, PRC President Hu Jintao sent a senior diplomat to Pyongyang to lean on the North Korean leader Kim Jong Il only after President Obama suggested that the United States would move warships to the seas off Chinese shores unless China had budged on the North

Korean nuclear issue. I personally heard President George W. Bush say on at least two occasions that China became more actively involved after he had talked directly with the Chinese Presidents (once to Jiang Zemin and the other time to Hu Jintao). In those circumstances, the United States took the position that it had no other choice but to resort to extraordinary (presumably military) measures if no progress was made on the issue.

However, China continues to emphasize the need to handle the North Korean nuclear issue through dialogue even though Beijing seems to have all but given up on the six-party talks which have been stalled for more than three years. Instead, it lends political support and diplomatic shields to North Korea. China does not want the Stalinist regime to collapse nor to waste an opportunity to increase its influence over it at a time when the new leadership after the death of Kim Jong Il badly needs support and embrace of China. By endorsing the third-generation dynastic succession of Kim Jong Un, China can easily issue an IOU it can use over North Korea later on. Nonetheless, in the aftermath of the demise of Kim Jong Il, China seems to be urging North Korea to refrain from continuing bellicose behavior including nuclear tests, rocket launches, and conventional provocations against the South as well as the rest of the world.

Japan feels threatened by North Korea's development of nuclear weapons and their delivery system. After the Geneva Agreed Framework was signed in 1994, Japan agreed to make a substantial financial contribution (a yen equivalent to one billion U.S. dollars) for the construction of light-water nuclear reactors in North Korea in return for the scrapping of the North's nuclear weapons and facilities program. However, Japan's ability to exercise influence on the negotiation process has been limited because of its obsession with the issue of North Korean abduction of Japanese citizens.

South Korea feels most threatened by the North's nuclear program for at least three reasons. First, should North Korea become a genuine nuclear weapons state, the military balance on the Korean Peninsula could fundamentally shift in favor of Pyongyang. Second, with all the neighboring countries being either nuclear weapons states or advanced in nuclear technology and material, South Korea would be left far behind the others in nuclear capabilities. Third, North Korea's nuclear status could trigger a domino of proliferation process in Northeast Asia which may increase the pressure for South Korea to reexamine its nonnuclear weapons policy.

South Korea agreed to take up the lion's share of cost for the construction of light-water reactors in North Korea to implement the 1994 Geneva Agreed Framework. South Korea is still concerned with the North becoming increasingly hostile and belligerent. This is occurring as Seoul is attempting to maintain a balanced relationship with Pyongyang, which over the years became spoiled by an indulgent and pliable South Korean government. In recent years, North Korea perpetrated conventional provocations against the South such as the sinking of a South Korean navy corvette and the artillery shelling of an island. At least verbally and indirectly, it continues to be intransigent and warlike after the death of Kim Jong Il. In the absence of any progress in solving the North Korean nuclear problem and in the face of an unapologetic attitude as portrayed by Pyongyang, the Lee Myung-bak administration could not provide large-scale assistance to the North during its five-year term which is to end in four months. In the meantime, the South Korean public is experiencing such severe fatigue with the nuclear issue and prolonged strain of relationship with the North that leaves a possibility open for whoever is elected in the Presidential election in two months (on December 19) to launch a new administration which is likely to adopt a more forthcoming and less rigid policy toward North Korea.

In any case, Japan and Korea, sitting on the same side of the fence with regard to the North Korean nuclear issue, are not completely satisfied with China's at best lukewarm attitude toward Pyongyang's nuclear program. Neither are they persuaded by the Chinese argument that, it has all the time grappled with the issue, and right now the priority task is to prop up the North Korean regime as well as its new leadership.

Rise of China and Resurgent Nationalism in Northeast Asia

Therefore, divergent perspectives and interests held by the three Northeast Asian countries make it difficult for them to cooperate and coordinate in their approaches to North Korea. Nevertheless, the three countries have no choice but to cooperate and coordinate with each other if they wish to deal appropriately with North Korea and its nuclear weapons program. Fortunately, the record shows that China normally does not link the North Korean issue to other issues that pertain to the three states. All our three nations should see to it that issues such as territorial disputes or trade disagreements would not spill over into their coordinated handling of the North Korean nuclear issue.

Second, the most serious obstacles to sub-regional integration in Northeast Asia are the resurgent nationalism and conflicting territorial claims. Sixty-seven years after the end of World War II, it is still unfortunate for the three nations to remain embroiled with nationalistic issues and territorial claims in particular. Why do we witness the seeming burst of nationalistic sentiments on top of a spate of territorial claims and disputes in recent years? I can put forward the following several explanations:

First, the rise of China and its consequent assertion of the rights to territories it claims are justifiably its own but had not been paid sufficient attention until recently while focusing on reforms, internal cohesion, and economic development. China now feels ready to retrieve what it considers were lost territories during the period of its weakness and underdevelopment. Just when refocusing its attention on what China considers either deprived or unsettled territorial claims, it sees Japan nullifying its claims and the United States checking and encircling it with alliances and alignments with China's neighboring countries. Despite the Japanese government's explanation that the nationalization of the disputed island of Senkaku/Diaoyudao was intended to preempt a move by some ultranationalists in Japan to purchase the islands, China regards the move as a direct and ultimate challenge to China's claims on them. Another element in Chinese behavior on this issue is its penchant to "teach a lesson" to its adversary and potential adversaries now as well as for a future China. Just as having gone to war against India (in 1962) and Vietnam (in 1979), ostensibly to teach these countries a lesson that they could not offend China without retribution, China wishes to send a signal to Japan and others, with which it is undergoing disputes with regard to the current territorial claims, that it would not tread softly on any territorial issues. Chalmers Johnson, an

American political scientist wrote a book entitled *Peasant Nationalism and Communist Power*, in which he argued that Mao Zedong's Communist movement succeeded on the back of peasant nationalism in China. The current Chinese leadership (the fifth generation since 1949) seems to carry on the tradition of legitimizing its government on the basis of nationalist credentials. Nationalism continues to be a potent force in Chinese politics as shown by the fact that demonstrators in the recent Senkaku/Diaoyudao dispute were seen carrying Chairman Mao's portrait.

China also seems to regard that behind the vigorous territorial claims of Japan (and for that matter in the South and East China Seas of such Southeast Asian countries as Vietnam and the Philippines) lie the support and encouragement given to those countries by the United States to defy China, particularly with its "rebalancing (pivot) to Asia" policy under the Obama administration. The Chinese leadership, which at the moment is in the process of transition, has both political motivation and necessity to take a strong stance on territorial issues. The United States on its part appears to confirm the fears and suspicions of China by its actions including the recent dispatch of aircraft carriers, *John Stennis* to South China Sea and *George Washington* to East China Sea.

Third, there have been sentiments rising in Japan that the deal it made after World War II as a defeated power, including the Peace Constitution and the abstinence of armed forces, is an anomaly that needs to be corrected and that Japan needs to be restored as a "normal state" with the right to possess defense forces and to exercise collective self-defense. The slowdown of Japanese economy for over two decades has caused the Japanese people a sense of relative decline vis-à-vis the other Northeast Asian countries such as China and Korea—a sense that seemed to have given further impetus as a result of the great tsunami-related disasters in March 2011. Such sentiments can easily stimulate a more nationalistic and assertive impulse.

Japan's feeling that its neighbors are attempting to take advantage of its relative decline and beginning to look down upon Japan is revealed not only by the ultranationalists but also among more ordinary Japanese, particularly of younger generations. They question why those generations of Japan who have nothing to do with the pre-World War II Japan's imperialistic and militaristic behavior should be responsible for what had happened at least two generations (seven decades and more) ago. They claim that Japan has made numerous apologies and sufficient financial compensations for its past misdeeds. They ask: How much more and for how much longer should Japan be making apologies and financial compensations? Why should Japan continue to maintain a Constitution that prevents, if not prohibits, it from maintaining regular defense forces and normal collective self-defense? Why should Japan feel guilty about possessing and wanting to possess territories that they consider are rightfully theirs?

Even as Japan desires to fight against the territorial challenges that China and Russia are presenting, its government recognizes that there are limits to what it can do in dealing with Russia which still is a military superpower as well as with China which is becoming an economic superpower. Russia has resumed its extensive sea and air military exercises around the Japanese archipelago, an act that Japan tends to underplay as being intended primarily vis-à-vis China. Pressed at home by nationalistic sentiments of the general public and some politicians, the Japanese government leaders find it politically necessary and useful to hammer on what it claims as a territorial dispute with Korea, a country that is neither militarily nor economically as formidable as either China or Russia.

Fourth, Japan's immediate neighbors which had been victims of Japanese imperialism and militarism feel that despite expressions of superficial regret and apology, Japan has not fully accounted for its misdeeds and the damage they suffered from the imperial Japan. Koreans are particularly upset by the Japan's refusal to officially acknowledge the wartime sex slavery and to apologize to and compensate the victims who are euphemistically called "comfort women." The South Korean Supreme Court ruled in 2010 that the (South Korean) government was negligent in implementing the relevant provisions of the Constitution to protect the rights of its citizens by not pressing the Japanese government more vigorously for apologies and compensations.

In the view of the Koreans, the island of conflicting claims, Dokdo (which Japan calls Takeshima) is not so much an issue of territorial claims as it is a problem of historical records because the island had been incorporated into Shimane-ken in 1905 in the course of Japan's colonization of Korea and as a result of the Japanese imperialistic designs. Korea is also sensitive to China's "Northeast Project" (albeit of Chinese scholarly circles) by which it is seen as an attempt to incorporate the ancient Korean history (of Gojoseon and Goguryeo) into that of China. All these nationalistic and territorial issues portend disagreements and conflicts.

Finally, the increasing availability of modern means of communication in recent years has contributed to galvanizing nationalism in the Northeast Asian countries. The explosive spread of electronic means of communication, including the Internet, cellular phones, and particularly SNS, has made nationalistic sentiments susceptible to fast and wide mobilization. No matter whether a state has democratic or authoritarian government, the leadership is subjected to enormous pressure of the public to act on nationalistic impulses while at the same time being tempted to use the territorial and nationalistic issues for garnering political support.

The problem is that, in galvanizing nationalism and exacerbating conflicts among nations in Northeast Asia, all these explanatory factors tend to reinforce one another and as such they seem to be activated all at the same time. Are the worsening relations among the three Northeast Asian countries on a slippery slope? Especially with leadership changes taking place in all the three countries and the prospect of an enlightened and strong leadership emerging in any of them not being bright, one may worry about the relations getting worse among the three countries without any brake or slowdown.

Regarding the role that South Korea can and should play in the triangular relationships among the three Northeast Asian countries, there are a number of views. They range from maintaining equidistance, tilting to one or the other, being friendly to both parties and, perhaps, even forming a three-country community or coalition, and playing the role of an equal competitor and, further, becoming a balancer of sort.

In the last configuration (balance of power), China would maintain an overwhelming economic link not only with the United States but also with Japan and South Korea. This assumes that, while China remains the largest trading partner with each of the major actors in the region, Korea will be closely tied with the United States, and with Japan militarily even though indirectly, and in terms of security. It also assumes that even as China's economic and military power grows, its economic interdependence with other countries will continue to dictate a cooperative Chinese policy with the other Northeast Asian states.

However, all of the above-mentioned policy alternatives are difficult, if not impossible, to implement or maintain because the three countries have different interests in and perspectives of a range of major issues. Clearly, in order to survive, navigate, and hopefully thrive in this turbulent neighborhood, Korea will have to adopt varying mixtures of the above alternatives according to the needs and dictates of times and circumstances.

In dealing with the North Korean nuclear issue, Korea finds its position closer to Japan's and hopes to bring China on their boards. On the alliance issue, the United States is clearly a linchpin that brings Korea and Japan together and encourages them for closer cooperation and collaboration. Both value their alliances with the United States, which China regards with a degree of misgiving. However, even though China does not readily admit it, their (Korea's and Japan's) alliances with the United States have an element of serving the interest of China as well. The alliances give Japan and South Korea a sense of security of reassurance so that they could be kept from excessive arming, including with nuclear weapons. In negotiating the extension of missile ranges, South Korea finds the United States being conscious of the interests, not only of Japan but also of China, as it tries to limit the range to 800 kilometers and the payload to within 500 kilograms. On the issues of pre-World War history involving Japan and of how the postwar generations have dealt with them, Korea finds itself sharing the views and sentiments with China more often than with Japan. It is only in the economic and trade areas that the three states, despite being competitors, find themselves sharing common interests.

Are there any mitigating factors, though, that could help restore and establish better and more cooperative relationships among the three?

First, there is the economic need to cooperate. As mentioned, the leaders of the three nations agreed in May 2012 to negotiate a trilateral FTA. The mutual attitudes (likes and dislikes) between the peoples of China, Japan and Korea are reasonably positive though not the best. Feelings between Koreans and Chinese as well as between Japanese and Koreans tend to be better than between Japanese and Chinese. The number of visitors, especially tourists, between and among the three countries is rapidly rising. The exchanges and cooperation in culture, tourism, and civil society are extensive and interwoven. Underneath the political and often hostile rhetoric, there is a decent sense and will in various sectors and layers of all the three societies, within and among the media, intellectuals, business people, and the general public. Second, the United States can play a positive role, especially in Korea-Japan relations. Despite Chinese misgivings, the alliances that the United States maintains with South Korea and Japan can help preserve and guarantee peace between its Northeast Asian allies and prevent further proliferation of nuclear weapons in the sub-region. So, one cannot say that the prospects for more positive relations among the three countries are only grim. All they should and can try is to maximize the positive elements and minimize the negative ones in their relations.

Most importantly, the three countries should take care so that the emotional and unsolvable territorial and nationalistic issues may not spill over to more pragmatic and businesslike issues of economic exchanges and cooperation including trade, investment, and finance. Furthermore, on functional issues such as environment and cultural and educational exchanges, cooperation and collaboration should be sought despite and beyond political conflicts. To this end, we need the enlightened leadership of all the three nations, which would lead their respective peoples to join in more pragmatic and productive cooperation.

To paraphrase Clemenceau, then French Prime Minister of the World War I years, who said, "A War is too important an enterprise to leave it entirely to the generals," the trilateral relationships among China, Japan and Korea are too important to be left to government leaders alone. The private sector, individual citizens, and all the nongovernmental organizations (NGOs) civil organizations—interest groups, cultural societies, educational institutes, and religious associations—should contribute to building more constructive, productive, and peaceful relationships to turn the uneasy triangle into an optimum one and hand it over to our subsequent generations.

Chapter 5

Division Management and Unification: Korea vs. Germany

Status of Inter-Korea Relations

Possibility for Duplication?

Persuading Major Powers

China's Interests and Reasons for Its Stance

Conclusion

Chapter 5

Division Management and Unification: Korea vs. Germany[76]

The German unification of 25 years ago still evokes admiration and envy among the Koreans. Before Germany was unified, the relationships between East and West Germany and those between North and South Korea had shared both similarities and differences. Both countries were divided by the occupation of separate Allied powers in the wake of World War II. Both countries turned into fields of East-West confrontation while being incorporated into the postwar alliance systems. In neither case, the surrounding powers seemed eager to have them unified. The neighboring countries to Germany feared that it might be reborn as a strong unified nation, whereas the countries around the Koran Peninsula were concerned about the possibly unstable aftermath of unification and the possibility for a unified Korea falling into some other nation's sphere of influence.

At the same time, there have been several differences between the German and Korean divisions. Five such differences stand out. For one

---

76. Keynote address at Conference on "International Cooperation for Korean Peaceful Unification," organized by the Unification Preparation Committee, November 26, 2015.

thing with the national division, while the Koreans were inflicted with what might be called "victim's complex," the Germans had what might be called a "guilt complex." Koreans had the sense that they had done nothing wrong to deserve the tragedy of division but were simply the victim of power politics and backdoor understanding between the powers, especially the United States and the Soviet Union. In contrast, the Germans recognized and accepted the fact that their national division was the result of what pre-World War II Germany had done; the invasion of neighboring countries, persecution of some ethnic groups, particularly the Jews, and precipitation of World War II.

Secondly, during the period of national division, while the DDR, East Germany, was under effective control and protection by the Soviet Union and so posed no serious military threat on West Germany by itself, North Korea was a constant security threat to South Korea, what with an all-out military invasion of the South which resulted in the Korean War, smaller scale military provocations including commando attacks, and the development of nuclear weapons and missiles of various kinds.

Third, while the fervor and activist movements for unification came mainly from younger generations and politically leftist sectors in Korea, the relatively subdued and passive calls and desire for reunification tended to derive from the older generations and more from the conservative sectors.

Fourth, while West Germany was an important member and active participant of multilateral regional and security organizations such as the European Community and NATO, South Korea's main security link to the outside world was a bilateral alliance with the United States and it enjoyed no membership in regional organizations or communities. So when the unification came to Germany, the East Germans were prepared to join not only their Western brethren and sisters, but also the European Community and NATO, thereby diluting the sense that East Germany was being taken over by West Germany.

Finally, after 45 years of the German division and 70 years of Korean division in 1945, there is a big difference in the nature of the relationship between East Germany and North Korea on the one hand and the Soviet Union and China on the other, their respective benefactors and guardians.

In 1990, the Soviet Union was a declining and disintegrating empire, in need of economic help from the outside after overspending in arms build-up and competition with the West, and in the process of internal transition from autocracy and dictatorship to perestroika and glasnost. In 2015, China is a rising economic power still under an effective one-party rule, challenging the domination of the United States and territorial status quo in East Asia, even as it has a strong interdependent relationship with the West and even though it has its own share of risks of rapid economic growth and self-aggrandizement. Nonetheless, East Germany was still under firm control of the Soviet Union and North Korea has been struggling for self-reliance and determination.

Status of Inter-Korea Relations

Roughly speaking, since the end of the Korean War in 1953, inter-Korea relations have gone through seven different phases with various degrees of hostilities and engagements. The post-Armistice period of 1953–60 can be characterized as one of internal recuperation from the war in both Koreas and estrangement between the two Koreas.

The second phase (1960–72) is one in which South Korea witnessed the emergence of a military government and North Korea became increasingly belligerent toward South Korea with occasional military (although small-scale) provocations both to South Korea and its ally the United States.

The third phase (1972–84) could be characterized as one of co-existence in that a series of dialogue got started as the two governments tried to use inter-Korea dialogue for the consolidation of power in their respective home fronts.

Dialogue sputtered through the fourth phase (1984–92) despite the North Korean attempt at assassination of the visiting South Korean president when the North Korean regime planted and exploded a bomb at the Aung San Mausoleum in Rangoon, Burma in 1983. In the late 1980s, faced with the collapse of the Soviet bloc and the unification of Germany, North Korea felt obliged to reckon with South Korea which was broadening its diplomatic horizon starting with the hosting of the 1988 summer Olympics and thus engage with South Korea in a serious bilateral dialogue. It resulted in such landmark agreement as Basic Agreement on Reconciliation, Non-Aggression, Exchanges and Cooperation (1991), and Joint Declaration on Denuclearization of the Korean Peninsula (1992) Agreement.

But the apparent lunge toward reconciliation was superseded by another, fifth, phase of estrangement (1993–98) as North Korean nuclear weapons program became a focal issue of contention. I was serving as South Korea's Foreign Minister during this period.

The sixth phase (1999–2008), that of "Sunshine Policy," was ushered in when Kim Dae-Jung, a long-time advocate of engaging the North became president in 1999. After his term of five-years was over, another "Sunshine Policy" president, Roh Moo-hyun, succeeded Kim for the next five-year term until 2008. But ironically during this period, North Korea resumed and accelerated its nuclear weapons development.

Thus, when the conservative government of Lee Myung-bak took office in 2009, the Sunshine Policy was replaced by a more balanced policy which was less unconditional, one-sided and indulgent toward North Korea. The seventh, and the current phase (2009 to date) of North-South Korean relationship can be characterized by continuing advancement of North Korean nuclear weapons program, a deteriorating economic condition of the North, and the start of a third generational dynastic succession process.

Possibility for Duplication?

Despite these differences between the divided Germany and Korea, however, South Koreans have been hopeful that they could duplicate the German path to unification. On the other hand, German unification provided North Korea with both incentives and perhaps means to prevent a similar process from taking place on Korean Peninsula.

In fact, North Korea had plenty to worry at the time of Germany unification: The Soviet empire was disintegrating; Both China and the Soviet Union officially recognized the Republic of Korea and established diplomatic relations with it, while the United States and Japan did not reciprocate for North Korea; the United States and the Soviet Union agreed on a détente; China and the United States agreed on a rapprochement;

and North Korea opposed the application of the German formula to Korea.

In that sense, German unification brought about retrogression rather than progress in the short term in the North-South Korean relationship by stiffening the North Korean attitude. This is a very tragic irony for a divided country. While both North and South Korea clamor for unification, neither side would think of turning over power to or sharing it with the other in the name of unification. Under such circumstances, a call for unification by either side would appear to the other as a desire to absorb or subjugate, if not conquer, the other. Thus, North Korea, as a means to prevent regime change, chose to develop WMDs including nuclear weapons and missiles and to further insulate itself from outside influence.

Since 2006, that is, during the last ten years, North Korea conducted three nuclear weapons tests and pursued what it named the *byongjin* policy, described as a parallel policy to become a nuclear weapons state while simultaneously reviving its economy.

In the meantime, the Park Geun-hye government that succeeded the Lee Myung-bak government pretty much continued the preceding government's "measured engagement policy" but with greater emphasis on cooperation with North Korea and search for "unification." The problem has been that the Park government had to overcome two hurdles to get positive results from its policy for promoting unification. One is the need to overcome North Korea's suspicion that Park's unification overtures are nothing less than a call for "unification by absorption," that is, by the German formula. The other is that it had to find a formula by which North Korea would suspend and then abandon its nuclear weapons program and refrain from conventional provocations.

Persuading Major Powers

Another important task for the Korean government is to persuade the four major powers, i.e., China, the United States, Russia, and Japan, that have strong interest in how the situation on the Korean Peninsula develops, that Korean unification, when and if it comes, will actually be in accord with their respective interests rather than being against them.

So, how will Korean unification affect their interests? One can think of both positive and negative interests of the major powers on Korean unification.

Let's first talk about the interest of the United States. There are some positive reasons why the United States will think Korean unification to be in its own interest as well.

Positive Reasons:

1. War in or over Korea less likely
2. North Korean threat (WMDs, missiles, etc.) and provocations removed
3. Emergence of a unified Korea as a powerful ally
4. Korea's increased dependence on the United States in the short term—need for economic and security support from the U.S.
5. Expansion of democracy, market economy

But there are also possible negative reasons why the U.S. could think Korean unification to be against its interest:

1. Weakening of rationale, necessity for the U.S.-Korea alliance
2. Korea' possible move closer into Chinese sphere of influence
3. Decrease in U.S. influence over Korea
4. Further deterioration of relations between Korea and Japan

Next, let's have a look at opposing reasons Japan may have for Korean unification.

Positive reasons:

1. North Korean threat (nuclear weapons, missiles, etc.) removed
2. Expansion of "free world" (democracy, market economy)
3. Korean preoccupation in internal matters during unification process
4. Increased need for Japanese support and help

Negative reasons:

1. Emergence of a powerful neighbor
2. Removal of Japan's rationale for militarization (against North Korean threat)
3. Loss of opportunity for "divide and rule" between North and South Korea
4. Possibility for a unified Korea to move closer to China

Russia may as well have contending reasons for welcoming or being reluctant for Korean unification.

Positive Reasons:

1. Increase in economic opportunities (gas, railroads, transportation, trade, investment, etc.)
2. Weakening of the U.S. alliance system
3. Assumption of a key role in the unification process

Negative Reasons:

1. Loss of opportunity to "fish in troubled waters" (between North and South Korea)
2. Possibility for increased Chinese influence over Korea

China's Interests and Reasons for Its Stance

A key factor in Korean unification would be what China thinks would portend for its own interest. What kind of calculus is China making in actuality about unification of the Korean Peninsula, and what role is it expected to play? Although we often speak of "China's thinking," no unified consensus seems to exist among the experts in China's North Korea policy directly concerning unification. Their views seem to diverge into several ramifications:

First is that China has to render unconditional assistance to its blood ally of North Korea and safeguard its security. Second is to maintain the present policy of shielding North Korea on the one hand and of recommending cooperative relations with other countries including Japan, South Korea, and the United States. The PRC wants to make the Pyongyang regime undertake reforms and refrain from provocations with a view to preventing military conflicts on the Korean Peninsula. The third view is to exercise stronger pressure on North Korea, partake in international sanctions, and abandon the defense of Pyongyang if necessary.

Among these three alternatives, the PRC government's current North Korea policy may be seen as the second, i.e. to encourage reforms, opening, and restraint from provocations while supporting the preservation of the DPRK and its regime survival.

China's North Korea policy, however, seems to have begun moving, though little by little, toward the third alternative, a policy of mounting pressure on North Korea. This is deemed to have a close relationship with China's calculation of interests in Korean unification and perception of North Korea's nuclear threat.

China thinks it would get the following short-term benefits should the Korean Peninsula be unified under the South Korean auspices:

First, if the peninsula is unified, China will be relieved from the burden of economic aid and military assistance for North Korea that has so far been greatly onerous.

Second, being relieved from hostilities and confrontations on the peninsula between North and South Korea, the PRC will become free from danger of military clashes and war it considers to be against its own interest.

Third, when unification under South Korea's initiative is premised, China will not only further expand and vitalize its economic relations that are already vibrant with the South but seize opportunities to secure its economic interests in the North Korean region in a stable manner.

In the longer term, Beijing may hope for the following benefits from Korean unification:

First, a major source of trouble and insecurity will have been removed. Second, a unified Korea will not merely offer a greater economic opportunity for China but contribute to regional integration as well.

Third, a unified Korea will obviate the rationale and necessity for external power's (meaning the U.S.) military presence regardless of developments in Sino-American relations. At the same time, the rationale for a ROK-U.S.-Japan trilateral alliance to contain and encircle China will be weakened.

Despite such positive short- and long-term implications, China also has apprehensions over negative consequences and impacts from unification of the Korean Peninsula.

In the short term, China is concerned as follows:

First, should the peninsula destabilize in the vortex of unification, innumerable refugees will flow from North Korea into China. While crossing the Yalu River and entering the border zones of China's two Northeastern (Jilin and Heilungkiang) provinces, North Korean refugees will flow along the sea lanes to land on the Liaoning, Tianjin, Shandong coasts. The massive influx of refugees will not only impose a tremendous financial burden on China but constitute threats to regional security. The refugee problem will also be a thorny issue in relations with a unified Korea.

Second, unification of the Korean Peninsula will cause a short-term negative impact on economic relations between China's three Northeast Provinces which account for 70 percent of China-North Korea trade.

In medium and long terms, China has the following concerns over the consequences of unification:

First, China will lose the presence of North Korea which can serve as a "buffer" to the U.S. presence in Northeast Asia.

Second, China's economic foothold in North Korea may shrink and weaken in the short term as South Korea will replace it. Although China-North Korea trade (approximately $6.5 billion in 2013) does not constitute a big share of China's annual external trade since it corresponds to an extremely miniscule portion (0.155% or 1/600) out of its total trade volume ($4.2 trillion), Korean unification would deal a sizeable blow at Liaoning and Jilin Provinces, in which Dandong and Yanji would suffer more severely.

Third, there are uncertainties contained in such issues as alliance relationship (the ROK-U.S. alliance) and foreign troops' presence in a unified Korea.

I have discussed China's positive as well as negative incentives regarding the unification of the Korean Peninsula. Let me now further elaborate on the issues I mentioned earlier regarding Chinese views on the ROK-U.S. alliance and the U.S. forces stationed in Korea.

Originally, until the end of the Cold War in the early 1990s, China had maintained a positive, or at least tolerant, position to consider as "necessary evil" not only the ROK-U.S. alliance but the U.S.-Japan alliance. The reason was that the U.S.-Japan alliance not merely had an effect of restraining Japan's rearmament (and nuclear armament, in particular) but played a role as well in checking the military power of the Soviet Union, which China considers a regional rival. China also recognized the value of the ROK-U.S. alliance playing a role of deterring North Korea's provocations on the Korean Peninsula.

As the Cold War ended and the Soviet threat largely died down, Beijing began to disparage the U.S. alliance system in Northeast Asia as a Cold War relic while judging that the ROK-U.S. and U.S.-Japan alliances targeted China.

China also stays vigilant against the possibility for such current bilateral arrangements as ROK-U.S. and U.S.-Japan alliances with the United States as their hub to develop into a NATO-type multilateral alliance.

Showing sensitive responses as well to the U.S. provision of extended deterrence ("nuclear umbrella") to Japan or South Korea, China retains an opposing position to it. China obviously thinks that the United States, by providing its nuclear deterrent to Japan and Korea, offsets or weakens China's own nuclear deterrent capability.

From an objective perspective, however, neither the U.S. extended deterrence nor the ROK-U.S. alliance is always disadvantageous to China. I think this is true both at present and even after Korean unification. The nuclear deterrence and the ROK-U.S. alliance, along with the U.S.-Japan alliance, will have an effect of continuing to bind Japan as a nonnuclear state. They will tend to obviate the need for arms expansion by evoking a reunified Korea's confidence in its security, and even arms reduction can further be expected as well. Furthermore, they will also enable the United

States to play a peacemaker's part between its allies, Japan and Korea, even after the Korean unification let alone now. At the same time, Korea will be able to assume a useful role as a constructive mediator for cooperation between the United States and China by maintaining close relationships with both great powers.

As far as the U.S. forces in Korea are concerned, China may expect that the justification or necessity could either diminish or disappear for their continued presence in the Korean Peninsula after unification. At a minimum, China may expect that the U.S. forces should not advance north of the present military demarcation line, even if the ROK-U.S. alliance is maintained and the U.S. troops continue to be stationed after unification. This may not be unacceptable to the ROK or the United State, although it is foreseen in the U.S. position that a certain level of direct U.S. military role is indispensable in the process of dismantling North Korea's weapons of mass destruction, especially nuclear arsenal and intercontinental ballistic missiles.

In consideration of long- and short-term interests as well as positive and negative reasons for China to be in favor of or against Korean unification, it may be worthwhile to keep in mind what China would consider as its "Red Lines."

First, South Korea and the United States must agree that the U.S. troops would not advance north of the demilitarized zone.

Second, the United States must not install a new military base north of the DMZ.

Third, as the ROK Army's activities in North Korea do not belong to a category of a war, they are beyond the scope of U.S. wartime operational control even before the OPCON is transferred. China may also wish the ROK forces avoid areas bordering China and retreat after disarming the North Korean army.

Fourth, South Korea and the United States must share with China the information including the "exclusive" information on North Korea.

Fifth, when securing North Korea's weapons of mass destruction (nuclear, biochemical arms and their delivery systems), the ROK-U.S. allies must allow international organizations such as the United Nations and IAEA to take charge of the procedures.

Sixth, China would insist on a unified Korea honoring treaties and agreements made with it (particularly regarding territories) by North or South Korea before unification.

Finally, a unified Korea must pledge to be a nonnuclear weapon state.

China emphasizes that unification of the Korean Peninsula should take place peacefully and "autonomously." PRC Chairman Xi Jinping visited South Korea early this month and also stressed in his lecture at Seoul National University that he supports "autonomous unification of the Korean Peninsula." It means that China opposes unification by war or military force and through North Korea's regime change intervened and initiated by a foreign country (i.e., the United States). At the same time, China generally seems to accept that unification under the Republic of (South) Korea's leadership is inevitable and it is a desirable consequence.

As above, I attempted to review China's interest calculation and roles in unification of the Korean Peninsula, but it may be viewed that there are meaningful changes in China's attitude in three respects:

One is the fact that China has recently conducted active researches and calculations with keen interest in unification of the Korean Peninsula and a lot of internal discussions are underway about China's interests and roles.

Second, it had until recently been regarded in the outside world that China is negative to a South Korea-led unification with a view to preserving North Korea as a buffer zone against the United States and South Korea. The truth, however, is that other variables and considerations are now interposed. For example, how much is North Korea a burden to China in economic, diplomatic, and security terms? How large a political burden does the North Korean regime's behavior levy on China? Are not there any aspects in which unification of the Korean Peninsula benefits China?

The third point is that China's attitude and policy toward unification could vary depending on our input in accordance with the aforementioned circumstantial changes, namely on what guarantee we would offer and what kind of picture depicting a post-unification Korea we would show to China.

Just like the case of German unification, it can be said that the possibility to realize unification of the Korean Peninsula would so increase as we attract the United States to actively support unification while assuaging Japan's unfavorable repercussions and having China accept Korean unification as palatable.

On the other hand, China is worried about the possibility for unification of the Korean Peninsula to influence the cross-strait relations between the mainland and Taiwan. The reason is that, according to the Chinese calculation, the possibility for a unified Korea to join an anti-China coalition front cannot be ruled out, and at the same time, Korean unification may as well pressure China's unification schedule.

All in all, China has greater concern about the journey than the destination to unification. The reasons include instability of North Korean society, the problem of refugees from the North, the possibility of armed clashes, and U.S. forces advancing to the North, which may occur (entail) in the process. It, therefore, will constitute a significant task for South Korea and the United States to assure China that the unification process would be peaceful, stable, and not disadvantageous to China.

It is necessary for us to dispel China's worries and satisfy its expected benefits as much as possible. For example, promising to honor the existing agreements (not only between South Korea and China but also between North Korea and China) would be an important measure to take.

When it comes to unification, not only China but also Japan, the United States, Russia, and so forth can calculate pluses and minuses to find both pros and cons for each of them. Focusing only on immediate interests, Russia probably has more reasons to welcome than to oppose Korean unification.

Nevertheless, as seen in the case of German unification, it would prove nearly impossible to convince China or Japan without the active cooperation and support from the United States. In promoting unification, it is essential for South Korea to consult and coordinate quietly but proactively with its four neighboring major powers.

Finally, let me say a few words about the North Korean nuclear weapons problem. North Korea's nuclear program and the erratic, unpredictable behavior of its new leader, Kim Jong Un, present a peculiar dilemma to South Korea and its neighbors. Thus far, the reactions of the concerned powers to the North Korean nuclear weapons threat seem to boil down to the following five strategies:

1. To pressure North Korea not to conduct more nuclear weapons or missile tests (as it stands now, focusing on preventing the fourth test)
2. To bring North Korea to a negotiating table such as the Six-Party Talks
3. To threaten with tougher and more stringent economic sanctions by the UN Security Council in case of additional tests of nuclear weapons or missiles
4. To threaten with punishments beyond UN sanctions
5. To offer inducements such as economic assistance and security guarantee in case North Korea abandons nuclear weapons

So far, none of these measures have shown to be effective in reducing, much less stopping, North Korean nuclear activities. Instead, North Korea's nuclear weapons program is looking increasingly more dangerous in terms of magnitude and capabilities. (Only two weeks ago, North Korea launched a long-range rocket, ostensibly for communication satellites but clearly for use as ballistic missiles.) North Korea's nuclear and missile programs are dangerous, not only to South Korea, but to all of the regional countries including China and Japan.

Thus, it may now be time for the United States and others to reexamine their "strategic patience" approach, which is tantamount to a recipe for inaction. The United States and South Korea should seek to cooperate and coordinate with the rest of concerned powers, i.e., China, Russia, and Japan, to work to roll back the North Korean nuclear program. Failing to limit the DPRK's nuclear development now means that its program will only get exponentially more dangerous in the years to come.

Conclusion

All the above interests of the major powers in Korean unification having been mentioned, it can be said just like in the case of German unification that possibilities for unification of the Korean Peninsula would increase as the United States could actively support Korean unification, Japan's unfavorable reactions could be assuaged, and China could accept Korean unification as palatable.

It would prove nearly impossible to convince China or Japan without active cooperation and support from the United States. In promoting unification, it is essential for South Korea to consult and coordinate quietly but proactively with its four major neighboring powers.

German unification was not initially welcomed by some of its neighbors including France and Great Britain as they regarded it to be against their interest. They were ultimately persuaded, mainly by the United States, to change their stance. It turned out that German unification ultimately turned out to be in the interest not only of the larger European Community and the individual countries in it but also of East European countries including the Soviet Union, later Russia. The unified Germany is the main source of energy and leadership in European integration, providing economic resources and serving as a bridge between the integrated Europe and the rest of it including Russia.

In the case of Korea, regardless of what each country considers Korean unification to be for or against its own interest, there are several selling points for a unified Korea. For one, it will be a sure way to solve the problem of nuclear weapons proliferation on the Korean Peninsula and in Asia at large.

Secondly, a unified Korea will surely contribute to peace and stability of the region by removing a critical source of tension and conflict.

Third, a unified Korea would become an economic powerhouse that would contribute to expanding economic scale, vitality, and activities in the region. It can also accelerate regional integration, peace, and prosperity by becoming a major basis and source of political and economic cooperation.

That is why all the interested parties, not only Koreans, should support and be in favor of the Korean unification.

Chapter 6

A Grand Strategy for South Korea?

The Regional Landscape: South Korea and the Major Powers

Strategic Choices

Conclusion

A Grand Strategy for South Korea?

All countries need a grand strategy. For the Republic of Korea (ROK), the nation's geopolitical position, the limits of its hard and soft power, and the division of the Korean Peninsula make it very difficult to formulate a practical or feasible grand strategy. Under the current circumstances, South Korea is limited in the range of key strategic options it can pursue. Formulating a grand strategy and implementing it is a challenge for any country. Even countries that are more powerful and occupy a stronger geopolitical position may find their ability to implement a grand strategy to be limited. The reasons for this can be attributed to any of the following: strategic planners' limited ability to know and accurately predict events and circumstances; false reasoning on intellectual, ideological, or psychological grounds; goal displacement by institutions or regimes; unexpected or unplanned outcomes; and rejection of the grand strategy as a result of unanticipated needs and/or obstacles that arise.

In the spring of 2018, several events, including a summit meeting between South Korean President Moon Jae-in and North Korean leader Kim Jong Un followed by one between Kim and U.S. President Donald Trump, seem to place the Korean Peninsula at the crossroads of reconciliation and peace on the one hand and conflict and war on the other.

North Korea decided to participate in the 2018 Winter Olympics held in Pyeongchang, South Korea, and the South Korean government, led by Moon Jae-in, turned it into an opportunity to hold summit meetings between conflicting parties in South and North Korea, the United States, China, and Japan. They discussed denuclearization, inter-Korean cooperation and exchanges, conflict reduction, and peace. Given the peculiarities of the leaders involved and the divergent interests of various parties, the series of diplomatic maneuvers by the leaders required deep strategic thinking and tact.

The task is particularly formidable for South Korea, as it seeks to maintain peace and security, economic prosperity, and political independence. It must navigate through the rough waters of ambitious and powerful neighbors, all of which have competing national interests.

Despite the difficulties, it is clear that South Korea must continue to engage in deep strategic thinking for both the present and future. In this regard, creating long-term strategies is highly important. A broad survey of strategic issues shows that South Korea may not have much of a choice when it comes to maintaining its alliance with the United States, actively engaging and cooperating with the rest of the world, or pursuing a balanced policy of accommodation and assertiveness toward its neighbors. However, the country has a greater range of options on certain issues. For example, there is more flexibility in South Korea's strategy for dealing with the competitive relationship between the United States and China, its troubled relationship with Japan, or its relations with North Korea.

South Korea must continue to develop its strategic thinking, as the process of formulating and reassessing strategies will inevitably produce better policies. This, in turn, will earn South Korea respect and trust from other countries, build greater coherence and confidence in the country's actions, and tackle larger tasks, such as unification. Finally, better strategic thinking will also contribute to greater understanding and unity among domestic constituencies within South Korea.

The Regional Landscape: South Korea and the Major Powers

The most pressing strategic issue for South Korea is how to position itself among the four most powerful nations in the region: the United States, China, Russia, and Japan. Therefore, to understand South Korea's strategic thinking, it is necessary to review the regional security landscape and several major developments that impact peace and security in Northeast Asia.

The first development is characterized by the rise of China and the emergence of what China describes as a "new type of major power relations." In other words, the geopolitical realities of the region, and the potential for conflict and cooperation, are highly influenced by two powers, the U.S. and China. With its growing economic power and military capabilities, China has begun to challenge the U.S.-dominated status quo and actively seeks to undermine parts of the international order that have existed since World War II. China seeks to reduce, if not end, the dominance of the U.S., especially in the Asian region. China is also determined to bring an end to U.S.-led alliances in Asia, which it considers Cold War relics. It has backed the establishment of the new Asian Infrastructure Investment Bank (AIIB) and has offered the countries in the region an alternative to infrastructure loans from the World Bank and Asian Development Bank (ADB). In effect, this directly challenges the power and influence of the U.S. in the fields of regional and international finance and banking. As a result, the conflict of interests between the U.S. and China is rapidly growing, and the two nations are increasingly in competition for regional influence, despite the need for cooperation in other aspects of their bilateral relations.

The second development is the growing tension and expansion of disputes between the U.S., on the one hand, and China and Russia on the other. This is exemplified by China's attempt to bring the South China Sea into its sphere of influence using confrontational tactics. China's actions included reclaiming land and building military facilities on Mischief Reef in the Spratly Islands, a move which faced strong opposition from the U.S., Japan, and neighboring Southeast Asian countries. The recent tensions with Russia have developed out of its actions in Ukraine. Russia's annexation of Crimea and military intervention in the Ukrainian conflict resulted in the imposition of economic sanctions against Russian individuals and companies by Western countries, to which Russia responded in kind.

A third major development is the warming of relations between China and Russia. Their growing disputes with the United States, and Russia's increasing isolation from the West, have brought China and Russia closer together. The two countries have embarked on ambitious oil and gas deals together, and their newly reinvigorated relationship prompted Russia to sign an agreement promoting China's New Silk Road initiative, after an initial response that was lukewarm at best. They have also concluded a significant arms purchase agreement, enabling China to acquire large amounts of advanced military hardware from Russia. In this marriage of mutual convenience and needs, China seems to be getting the more advantageous end of the deal. Russia has committed to supplying China with low-cost energy to meet its growing demands, and Beijing has also seized the opportunity to purchase weapons that make up some 60 percent of its arms imports.

Some observers argue that the simultaneous U.S. antagonism towards the two major world powers will push them to build a new political and military alignment, if not an alliance. But others assert that, because of the unequal nature of relations between Beijing and Moscow and the lack of trust between them, the chances of their forming a closer relationship are quite limited. Political scientist Joseph Nye, for example, recently stated that Russia is unlikely to be able to manage an alliance with China because "Russia's economic and military power has been in decline, whereas China's has exploded."[77]

Another reason precluding closer ties is the demographic imbalance between the sparsely populated Russian Far East and the densely populated Chinese territory across the border. A third factor that supposedly prevents closer ties is Russian unwillingness to become excessively dependent on China. Finally, experts argue that there is a fundamental lack of strategic trust and abundance of mutual suspicion, which will exclude the possibility

---

77. Joseph Nye, "A New Sino-Russian Alliance?" 2015. http://udenrigs.dk/new-sino-russian-alliance/.

of building a lasting partnership.

Whatever the case may be with the Sino-Russian coalition, the continuing development of a stronger relationship will have a negative effect on U.S. ability to cooperate closely and productively with them in dealing with such critical issues as the North Korean nuclear and ballistic missiles threat. It will also affect the U.S. ability to work with the two countries on trust-building and the establishment of a regional peace mechanism.

A fourth factor that affects the regional situation is related to the ambivalence of the U.S. policy toward Asia. The Obama administration characterized its policy towards the Asia-Pacific region as that of "rebalancing," which meant assigning a higher priority to political, economic, and security resources committed to the region. The main driver appeared to be the geopolitical realities of a rapidly rising China and the perceived need to respond. One of the fundamental elements of the policy was to strengthen relationships with allies and partners, including emerging powers such as India and Indonesia. These strategic plans were being implemented even as the U.S. continued to tighten its military budget.

In essence, the "turn to the East policy" continued with the Trump administration. Recently, the U.S. has been strengthening its alliances with Australia, Japan, and South Korea. It has assigned more resources to the region because of the perceived dynamism, opportunities, and challenges. The Trump government has begun to bring India into the coalition, emphasizing its new "Indo-Pacific strategy." The policy has attempted, with some success, to embed the United States in the emerging political, security, and economic architecture, including the East Asia Summit (EAS) and strengthen linkages of the U.S-Pacific-Indian Ocean crescent. The policy even seeks to establish a more extensive and structured relationship with ASEAN.

At the same time, rather than focusing on the containment of China, the U.S. has tried, with limited success, to maintain a positive and stable relationship with Beijing. A strategic policy that furthers cooperation and manages tensions in this bilateral relationship has been seen as more favorable than one that fosters competition and conflict. However, in the course of implementing its new Asia policy, the U.S. has been forced to turn its attention away from the region and expend energy elsewhere, such as the Middle East and Europe. Subsequently, the continuing troubles in these regions have made it difficult for the U.S. to pivot away.

The pivot to Asia policy has also encountered difficulties due to Chinese suspicions of U.S. intentions. China believes the real U.S. objective is to maintain its position of supremacy in Asia and contain China. Russia has also reacted to the U.S. policy by "turning to," if not "rebalancing to," the Northeast Asian region. Russia must also deal with a rising China seeking to impose its will on territorial issues, and intensifying maritime and territorial disputes in the East and South China Seas. Moscow sees Beijing as being prepared to use its growing economic leverage to counter America and expand its own sphere of influence.

A number of China's neighbors likewise see the country's rising power as a threat and believe that China will utilize its military to enforce its territorial claims. They worry that China will use its economic leverage to diminish their response options, and so they have sought out American reassurance and support. This, in turn, has persuaded Beijing that the U.S. is orchestrating a plan to create increased regional opposition toward China in order to isolate and contain the country.

With regards to Japan, the U.S. is closely cooperating with Prime Minister Abe's government to implement its Asia policy. Japan has revised the interpretation of its Peace Constitution to make "collective self-defense" possible. The government has agreed on new "defense guidelines," enacted through legislation in the National Diet, which will allow the use of Japanese forces beyond the defense of the archipelago proper. The new U.S.-Japan Defense Guidelines adopted in April 2015 state that the Self-Defense Forces will conduct appropriate operations involving the use of force to respond to situations where an armed attack against a foreign country that is in a close relationship with Japan occurs. Japan is also collaborating closely on a ballistic missile defense (BMD) project, and it has been working in tandem with the U.S. to denounce China's territorial expansion schemes in the South China Sea.

The United States regards Japan as a much more willing partner to deal with disputes with China than its other close regional ally, South Korea. This is because South Korea takes a somewhat less confrontational approach towards China. Even though South Korea has also been strengthening its alliance with the U.S. on a range of issues, it has taken a more circumspect approach than Japan in disputes between the United States and China for several understandable reasons.

First, as a divided country facing the North Korean threat of conventional weapons and weapons of mass destruction (WMDs), South Korea regards China as a key country with which it must actively pursue coordination. Second, it wishes to find the most effective and pragmatic way to deal with the Chinese challenge without unnecessarily and excessively antagonizing Beijing. Third, because of the enormous economic interdependence with China, South Korea is much more vulnerable to Chinese economic pressure than Japan is. Finally, it believes that the best way to maintain peace, harmony, and cooperation in the region is to find common ground and interests, to engage in dialogue and trust-building, and to diminish mutual suspicions and harsh rhetoric.

The United States, from its perspective, has a distinct need to maintain closely coordinated alliance relationships with both Korea and Japan to counter China's rising power and the North Korean threat. At the same time, it must acknowledge and respect each country's policies towards China and North Korea. This makes it difficult to carry out a comprehensive "rebalancing" policy and often strains relations among the three countries.

Turning back to the larger strategic picture in the region, a fifth development has to do with the troubled and deteriorating relationship between Japan and Korea. Close neighbors, the two throughout history have had a checkered relationship of competition, cooperation, and occupation. The most recent example of this troublesome past was the Japanese colonial domination of Korea for 35 years in the first half of the twentieth century. Seventy years after the end of World War II and Korean liberation from Japanese occupation, they have yet to throw off the shackles of the past and move beyond the legacies of previous historical misdeeds and grievances.

In particular, the two countries still dispute the factual record of "comfort women," or those young women who were forced into sexual slavery by the Imperial Japanese Army in the occupied territories before and during World War II. Seoul and Tokyo still have not agreed on a permanent resolution to this dispute because they are unable to find a satisfactory method for compensating the comfort women victims. There have been previous attempts, but Japan complains that Koreans are never satisfied with Japanese apologies and keep moving the goalpost for a final resolution. Koreans complain that Japanese apologies are never sincere or sufficient and that Japanese leaders keep making statements that are offensive to and dismissive of Koreans.

From the U.S. standpoint, quarrels between its two Asian allies are a vexing problem, adversely affecting the collaboration not only between them, but among all three countries. It also tends to make Korea and China strange bedfellows, both of which have unsettled grievances toward Japan. It has been 50 years since Korea and Japan normalized their diplomatic relations. There is still hope in both countries that Koreans will adopt a more generous and magnanimous frame of mind to forgive past historical misdeeds, and the Japanese will undertake a more sincere and deeper reflection of the past and present a way to resolve the issue of accountability. If this happens, the two countries may finally be able to establish common ground for greater understanding, cooperation, and lasting friendship.

Finally, North Korea's nuclear program and the erratic, unpredictable behavior of its young leader, Kim Jong Un, present a peculiar dilemma to South Korea and its neighbors. This has increased the security risk on the Korean Peninsula by raising the possibility of sudden change in North Korea. It has also driven the United States to strengthen U.S.-South Korea alliance capabilities. Still, the unresolved question is how to deal with North Korea's nuclear weapons program, which has become ever more intractable over the years. Since Kim Jong Un assumed the leadership, North Korea has not only codified in the preamble of its constitution that the DPRK is a nuclear weapons state, but it also officially adopted a two-track *byungjin* policy for simultaneous development of nuclear weapons and the economy.

In the face of North Korea's continued provocations and adamant refusal to engage in real diplomacy, there is among the Six-Party Talks countries a palpable sense of fatigue and resignation. Nonetheless, the recent Iran deal that lifts economic sanctions in exchange for curtailing their nuclear weapons program seems to have provided renewed momentum for a deal on the North Korean nuclear issue.

Despite occasional lulls in tension and North Korean gestures of possible accommodation, North Korea shows no sign of slowing down, much less dismantling its nuclear and missile capabilities. It may thus be the time for the United States and others to reexamine their patience, strategic or otherwise, and seek to coordinate with the other concerned powers, i.e., China, Russia, and Japan, to work to roll the North Korean nuclear program back in earnest. Failing to limit the DPRK's nuclear development now means that its program will only get exponentially more dangerous in the years to come.

It has been a quarter-century since the Cold War ended. East Asia has moved from a period when international relations were primarily dominated by the U.S.-Soviet bipolar power structure to a unipolar situation in which the United States maintained control over the region through its hegemonic position. Recent years have brought about another shift, which can be described as an emerging G2 structure, plus an evolving balance of power. East Asia today has a situation in which the continental powers of China and Russia are on one side, and the United States and Japan, essentially maritime powers, are on the other. South Korea is leaning heavily towards the maritime coalition, and North Korea remains isolated but leaning towards the continental powers. However, this divide is not like the one the world experienced during the Cold War. There is still time to seek cooperation among all the powers on a range of issues and create a regional architecture for peace, security, and prosperity. It would be in Korea's interest if trust can be built not only between the United States and China, but also between Russia and the United States, Japan and China, Japan and Korea, and even between North and South Korea. All these actors are heavily interdependent on one another economically, a fact which both necessitates and enables countries to seek cooperation and peace in the region.

Strategic Choices

Where does the newly emerging regional security landscape leave South Korea? What role can and should it play? The following is a summary of the various strategic options that South Korea may pursue, split into eight different threads, in some cases with overlapping and conflicting policy prescriptions.

1. Tilting: Because Korea is a peninsular country, there has been a debate as to whether its course should be that of a continental or a maritime power. Leaning towards becoming a maritime country would mean aligning itself more closely with the United States and Japan, whereas identifying itself as a continental power would mean placing greater emphasis on relations with China and Russia. Given the need to maintain amicable relations with all four, tilting is neither realistic nor practical.

2. Balancer: Roh Moo-hyun, president from 2003 to 2008, advocated that Korea be the regional balancer between China and Japan, a role somewhat akin to that which the United Kingdom played in the European balance of power in the eighteenth and nineteenth centuries. This policy was criticized at home as being unrealistic and pretentious, but it reflected the growing sense of self-confidence in a more assertive Korean nation and the desire to reclaim ownership of foreign relations.

3. Equidistance: This is a policy that is similar to that of a balancer, except that it does not call for Korea to "tilt" in either direction on regional issues in order to keep regional relations balanced. Given the multiplicity of issues that require joining forces with one nation or the other, this strategy may be impractical for Korea to pursue in any consistent and meaningful way.

4. Hedging: This is a policy of cultivating a fallback position and ultimately going with the prospective winner. Hedging is more dynamic and flexible than maintaining a balance or keeping equidistance between countries. As such, it could be seen by friends and adversaries alike as being opportunistic, unreliable, and untrustworthy. It is a strategy that is likely to subject the country to greater pressure from outside powers. One example of this is when South Korea adopted a policy of "strategic ambiguity" on THAAD. The only possible advantage of a hedging strategy

would be that the country does not need to be tied to a particular power or group of countries and, thus, would retain a degree of flexibility and freedom of choice. But the cost of flexibility far outweighs its benefits.

5. Bridge: This is a policy based on the assumption that Northeast Asian countries should minimize conflict and maximize cooperation, and that Korea could be a harmonizer among the major powers. Since Korea is situated between the major powers not only geographically, but also in economic development, temperament, and culture, the proponents of this strategy will argue that Korea can play a bridging role among the powers. However, given the large gap in interests and objectives of the powers, there are limits to the bridging role that Korea could play, even if it chose to do so.

6. Equal Competitor: This is a policy predicated upon the belief that South Korea has reached a level where it can stand alongside its neighbors and deal with them as equals. It does not assume that Korea is indeed equal in economic prowess, diplomatic clout, or population, but argues that Korea's growth has now put it at a level where it is not a "shrimp amid whales." The argument for this policy is also a reflection of growing Korean self-confidence and self-esteem.

7. Community: This policy is based on the belief that the three Northeast Asian nations have enough shared interests and commonalities that they can form a community. Community building can start with integration and cooperation in economics (a three-country free trade agreement, for example), the environment, and cultural exchanges. Such a community could be built on the shared culture and common interests of the countries of the region.

8. Status Quo (Balance of Power): According to this view, the current situation in which South Korea and Japan are allied with the United States, and China is aligned with Russia and supportive of North Korea, is an acceptable power configuration in Northeast Asia, even if not the most preferable one. In this configuration, China maintains strong economic relations not only with the United States but also with Japan and South Korea. This view assumes that while China remains South Korea's largest trading partner, the ROK will stay closely tied to the United States and

Japan for security and political relations. It also assumes that even as China's economic and military power grows, its economic interdependence with other countries will continue to dictate a cooperative Chinese policy with the other Northeast Asian states.

Conclusion

The above review of South Korea's strategic options shows that the country may have a range of choices when it comes to determining policy in different issue areas. When examining strategy in the context of the broader regional security landscape, however, the picture becomes less clear. One can see that the formulation of a grand strategy is nearly impossible because South Korea's different policy prescriptions are extremely difficult or impossible to establish and maintain. None of the choices are exhaustive, mutually exclusive, or permanent. The United States, China, South Korea, and Japan have different interests in and perspectives on a range of issues, but that should not prevent South Korea from pursuing the development of strategic thoughts and plans. The policy options discussed above are possible choices, but South Korea does not need to choose only one right now. Rather, it is important to think about and discuss when, in what sequence, in what combination, and which strategic option(s) to choose. In order to survive, navigate, and thrive in this turbulent neighborhood, Korea will have to adopt varying mixtures of the above alternatives according to the needs and dictates of time and circumstances. This should drive strategic thinkers in South Korea and other countries in the region to diligently create new options or to reassess those strategies already in place. The increased reliability and consistency of policies formulated out of this strategic thought process will lead to greater trust-building and cooperation among countries in the region.

As important as which strategic option(s) to choose is in what way and to what extent the strategy is formulated and how the policies are pursued. A strategy needs constancy without being rigid, flexibility without being void of direction, and thoroughness without being extreme. The leaders creating such strategies and policies should have convictions and principles but need to remain open to communication and opposing views.

Afterword

Koreans are used to being on the brink of both war and peace, although war often seems more imminent than peace. Sometimes a devastating war does take place. Other times they avoid it, by luck, fortitude, or skillful maneuvering (i.e., diplomacy). Yet even when war occurs, they somehow recover from the devastation and maintain their identity, as they did after the Korean War of 1950–53. This is why Koreans have sayings like, "Even if heaven tumbles down, there's always a hole to soar through." This is also probably why, to foreigners who observe them, Koreans seem surprisingly sanguine, if not nonchalant, in the face of missile and artillery threats from only 40 kilometers north of Seoul, where more than 10 million people live.

South Koreans disagree a lot about important questions: How great is the danger to the country at any given time? Who are our enemies and who are our friends? How benign or malignant are our adversaries' intentions? What to do about the dangers all around us? How can we make, secure, and build peace? Regardless, to survive and thrive, separately or together, we need skillful and robust diplomacy.

But just as Korea has serious and difficult diplomatic challenges, its ability to conduct effective diplomacy is limited by the circumstances in the region and conditions of their own making. Korea is a divided country between the North and the South, who in the last century fought a devastating internecine war, despite sharing the same ethnicity, language, and culture. Although there are occasional charades of peace and reconciliation, they are armed against each other and are still at each other's throats as proxies of more powerful outside powers.

Aside from the basic goals of policies, strategy may also involve the way (manner and style?) in which the goals are pursued. In recent years (2017–19), there were two instances in which South Korea mismanaged the triangular diplomacy. The first was the so-called "THAAD deployment" case and, the second, the "GSOMIA" crisis.

Afterword

In the first instance—that of the THAAD, in 2017, the United States wanted to deploy three battalions of THAAD (Terminal, High Altitude, Air Defense) missiles in Korea to defend the U.S. troops stationed in Korea from in-coming high altitude missiles from North Korea. China objected, arguing that it compromises China's offensive and deterrence missile capabilities. From the beginning, South Korea held an ambivalent attitude, saying that it neither had no discussions with the United States nor made any decisions on the issue. China added heavier pressure on Korea day by day. The result was eventual decision by the ROK government to allow the THAAD deployment which brought upon hurting economic sanctions and retaliation by China to inflict a heavy pain to the Korean economy and people. South Korea even committed itself to the so-called "three-don'ts"— not to allow deployment of additional THAADs, not to join the U.S.-led MD (missile defense) system in the future, and not to become a member of a defense pact consisting of the United States, Japan and South Korea.

The second instance was that of "GSOMIA" (General Security of Military Intelligence Agreement). In 2015, South Korea entered a three-year agreement with Japan (renewable after three years) to collaborate and exchange on critical military intelligence such as subway movements and missile firing and flights. However, when the South Korean government acted on a Korean court ruling on a wage dispute allowing it to confiscate assets of certain war-time (World War II) Japanese industrial companies, the Japanese government imposed an export ban on some strategic goods from being exported to Korea. The Korean government in retaliation announced and informed that it would terminate the three-year old GSOMIA when its three-year term would end in February, 2019. The United States, which had encouraged the two disputing countries to sign the intelligence cooperation pact as it would greatly benefit the three countries—U.S., Japan and South Korea—in their handling of the North Korean threat, became much agitated. As the United States urged South Korea to rescind its GSOMIA termination decision, what started out as a bilateral dispute became a critical trilateral issue. Even though the issue was temporarily resolved with South Korea withdrew ("tentatively") its decision to terminate GSOMIA with Japan, South Korea's loss of face as well as credibility by the allies was not insignificant.

In Korea, it is customary to say in one's thank you note at the end of your tenure as a government official that you are grateful to your colleagues for their help so that "no major mishap happened during my tenure." I used to think that that was much too modest and conceited a goal for a responsible official. At the same time, one does realize how lucky one is if he or she could leave office without a major mishap. Is it because disasters and mishaps happen so often in Korea, or because they were averted by your able and astute stewardship?

Ultimately, I think it has to do with the timing of your service. But what you do and how you perform your (diplomatic) duties do matter. And, in turn, this is related to how you approach problems and challenges and make the best use of the opportunities and resources that are available.

I have learned three things from the experience of handling diplomacy during a period when the country was on the brink of war: 1) You need to think pragmatically, free from time-worn ideology, emotions born of historical legacy, and domestic political constraints in order to work towards consensus and bipartisanship; 2) You need balanced thinking, being proud and independent-minded, but also being able to compromise and accommodate; 3) You need to be realistic and smart, recognizing that you cannot deal with challenges with courage and ardor alone.

Index

A
Agreed Framework	87, 88, 108~110
APEC diplomacy	22
Asian Games	22

B
Baekje	16
Brzezinski, Zbigniew	10
Bush, George W.	109

C
Carter, Jimmy	50, 53~55, 60~66, 71, 72, 74, 75, 78, 87
Chang Myon	43
China, or People's Republic of China (PRC)	20, 22, 50, 51, 73, 77, 97, 108, 127, 131
Chinese Communist Party (CCP)	17
Chinese dynasties	16, 106
Chinese government	22
Kuomintang (KMT)	17
Ministry of Foreign Affairs	22
one-China policy	23
South China Sea	112, 138, 141
Chun Doo-hwan	35, 61, 65~68, 72, 74
Clinton, Bill	30, 82
conference diplomacy	22
Combined Forces Command (CFC)	58, 67

D
demilitarized zone (DMZ)	19, 130
de-Stalinization campaign	20
Dulles, John Foster	34

F
four colonies (Hansagun)	16

G
Goguryeo	16, 114
Goryeo	16
Great Leap Forward movement	20

H
Han Dynasty	16
hijack diplomacy	22
Hwang Jang-yop	25, 88

J
Japan	9~11, 13, 17, 23, 26, 27, 31, 34, 35, 37, 39, 40, 43, 44, 51, 55, 56, 59, 66, 68~70, 73, 77, 81, 83, 84, 86, 88, 91, 93~96, 100~102, 104~116, 123~125, 127~130, 132~134, 137, 138, 140~147, 149
Japanese government	113, 149
Japanese imperialism	113
Jiang Zemin	24, 109
Johnson, Lyndon B.	46, 47
Joseon	16

K
Kanter, Arnold	81
Kim Dae-jung	65, 123
Kim Il Sung	17, 20, 55, 72, 87, 98, 99
Kim Jong Il	108~110
Kim Jong Un	89, 90, 92, 109, 133, 136, 143
Kim Yong Sun	81
Kim Young-sam	24, 30, 82, 83, 87
Koreagate scandal	43, 52, 60
Korean Armistice	19, 25, 27, 41
Korean War	9, 17~20, 25, 33, 37, 41, 62, 81, 83, 98, 121, 122, 148

L
Lee Chae-Jin	18
Lee Chong-sik	37

M

Mao Zedong	17~19, 112
Ming	16
Monroe Doctrine formula	34
Moon Jae-in	88, 89, 92, 136, 137

N

NATO formula	35

O

Oberdorfer, Don	21
Olympic Games	22

P

Park Chung-hee	43, 46, 48, 49, 57, 59~61, 63, 64, 72
Park Geun-hye	124
Pyongyang	9, 20, 21, 23, 25, 30, 55, 71, 81, 83~88, 95, 96, 99, 100, 108~110, 127

Q

Qian Qichen	23, 85
Qing	16
Quirino, Elpidio	40

R

Reischauer, Edwin O.	32
Roh Moo-hyon	123, 145

S

sadae juui	37
Scalapino, Robert A.	8
Seventh Fleet	18, 19
Shilla	16
Sino-American accommodation	23
Sino-American rapprochement	19
Sino-Japanese War	16
Sino-Soviet conflict	21, 99
South Korean model	23
Soviet Union	11, 17, 19~21, 23, 26, 32, 37, 38, 50, 51, 54, 62, 68, 69, 73, 75, 77, 81, 99, 107, 121~123, 129, 134

Stalin   17~19
Sung   16

T

Taedong River   30
Taiwan Straits   18, 19
38th parallel   18, 32
torpedo boat diplomacy   22
Treaty of Shimonoseki   16
Tumen River   18
two-Koreas policy   9, 23

U

United Nations (UN)   18~20, 22, 41, 58, 73, 85, 86, 88, 107, 130

    Security Council   20, 85, 86, 90, 91, 133
United States (U.S.)
    administration   64, 74, 78
    Air Force   54, 67, 71
    alliance system   105, 126, 129
    Congress   52~54, 68
    involvement   33, 35, 67
    Justice Department   52, 53
    policy   27, 71, 75, 102, 140, 141
    security commitment   26, 35, 40, 44, 49, 51, 68
    troop   27, 33, 44~46, 50~52, 81, 84, 92, 93, 95, 130, 149
    troop withdrawal   50, 53
USS *General Sherman*   30

V

Vietnam triangle   11

Y

Yalu   18, 19, 128
Yuan   16

Z

Zagoria, Donald   11